uthors *stand*

ractical *work*

this bo *s and*

—Stephanie Smith Lee, Former Director
Education Programs, U. S. Department of Education
Oakton, VA

"This book is a wonderful resource for anyone trying to navigate the complexities of supporting and advocating for disabled students in inclusive classrooms. The authors remind us that beneath our roles as professionals and parents we are all people who can find ways to sidestep—or dance—around many of the missteps that lead to misunderstanding and conflict."

—Emma Van der Klift and Norman Kunc, Co-directors
Broadreach Training and Resources
British Columbia, Canada

"This book serves as a vital resource and provides essential viewpoints for professionals. The text also reminds parents how valuable their input is to the process. In the spirit of collaboration, we highly recommend this book."

—Tiiu Presutti, Special Education Teacher
—Melinda Sulzbach, School Social Worker
—Adrienne Hershfield, School Psychologist
Montgomery Elementary School
Montgomery, NY

"I will use this book as a key text in my courses that include the topics of collaborative teaching, home-school partnerships, and conflict mediation. What a great book for modeling for new teachers the realities of collaboration in the IEP process and the best practices that make the process a joyful dance rather than a difficult experience."

—Jacqueline Thousand, Professor
School of Education, CSU San Marcos
San Diego, CA

A mother who found her calling through fate or accident—and never looked away or glanced back—Janice Fialka is internationally renowned for her relentless, never-say-never advocacy. She and her coauthors offer hope and wisdom for parents who would see more clearly into the lives of their children—disabled or not—and for every professional who would engage them.

—Bill Ayers, Distinguished Professor of Education, retired
Author, *To Teach: The Journey of a Teacher and A Kind and Just Parent*
University of Illinois
Chicago, IL

"Rarely does a book hold such promise for promoting genuine partnerships between families of children with disabilities and the professionals who participate in their care. The real-life passages from the authors, seasoned parents, and experienced professionals infuse this work with unparalleled authenticity."

—Susan Addison, MEd, Special Educator, retired
Chattanooga, TN

"The authors get right to the heart of parent-professional relationships. They deconstruct and reconstruct the difficult process of examining how parents and professionals communicate. The stories used to illustrate specific points are superb. We need this thoughtful and provoking perspective to encourage us to listen more closely to one another for the benefit our children."

—Martha E. Mock, PhD, Assistant Professor
University of Rochester
Rochester, NY

"If parents and professionals could wear out their shoes by dancing the way Fialka, Feldman, and Mikus describe it in this book, the shoes would indeed be worth pressing against one's heart. Through stories, the authors expertly choreograph the steps that families, professionals, and children must take to foster this essential relationship—like a waltz: one, two, three."

—Robin McWilliam, Director
Center for Child and Family Research, Siskin Children's Institute
Chattanooga, TN

"This book accomplishes two impressive feats. First, it conveys, through information and examples, research-based practices for building family-professional partnerships. Second, the clear, storytelling style of writing makes it impossible to put down. This is a must for anyone whose responsibilities involve working with the families of children with disabilities."

—Pamela J. Winton, Senior Scientist and Director of Outreach
FPG Child Development Institute, University of North Carolina
Chapel Hill, NC

"The authors powerfully illustrate the 'dance of partnership' in complex and nuanced ways. They capture how things are in the real world of relationships between parents and professionals. The stories are moving, the perspectives offer insights, and practical strategies and suggestions abound. I recommend this book as a superb source of guidance and support."

—Shari Saunders, PhD, Clinical Associate Professor
University of Michigan
Ann Arbor, MI

"This is a book written with a quality that is both honest and sensitive. The authors force us to put aside all other issues, reminding us what is real and essential in our pursuit of genuine student learning."

—Georgina M. Terrigno, MA, CCC/SLP, Speech and Language Pathologist
Monroe Woodbury Central School District
Central Valley, NY

"Having attended many challenging problem-solving meetings, I know how important it is for families and professionals to keep open hearts and minds. This unique resource moves beyond the 'how to's' of efficient and effective communication and reminds us of the values that are central to any great team—generosity, creativity, and a willingness to learn from one another."

—Paula Kluth, PhD, Consultant, Advocate
Author, *You're Going to Love This Kid: Teaching Students with Autism in the Inclusive Classroom*
Oak Park, IL

"This book's valuable information and insights make it a 'must read' for everyone involved in the special education process. I will refer to this book frequently as it reminds me of the often unsaid feelings and concerns of parents. The authors provide numerous useful approaches so that all parties can collaborate and do what is best for the child."

—Jacqueline Rau, 5th Grade Special Education Teacher
Maybrook Elementary School, Valley Central School District
Maybrook, NY

"Brilliantly written from the differing vantage points of both parents and professionals, this book shows how perceptions and assumptions can be falsely formed between 'opponents.' Use this knowledge to develop the strong partnerships necessary for parents and professionals to collaborate and support the needs of students!"

—Kathy Brill, Board Member
Parent to Parent USA
Mechanicsburg, PA

"So often in special education, the people involved share the same goal, yet envision a different path to achieve that goal. Fialka, Feldman, and Mikus remind us that our ultimate goal is the same. They show us how, even in the most difficult situations, we can 'dance' together in successful collaboration."

—Tara Rounds, School Psychologist and CSE/CPSE Chairperson
Haldane Central School District
Cold Spring, NY

"This book offers important suggestions for finding a way to dance together, reminding us exactly why we are dancing—for the child. I strongly recommend this text to parents and professionals. The real-life examples will help all parties understand and empathize with each other, making it that much easier to dance together."

—Jo Spahr, IEP Committee Member, retired, and parent of a college student with a disability
Valley Central School District
Newburgh, NY

"The parent-professional relationship can be awkward, so using the metaphor of learning to dance together to benefit children is apt. With the resources to help children shrinking, it is more vital than ever for parents and professionals to forge strong partnerships. This perspective can really help—highly recommended."

—Robert A. Naseef, PhD, Psychologist and father of an adult child with autism
Author, *Special Children, Challenged Parents*

"Fialka, Feldman, and Mikus have done the near impossible—they have described the process of partnership in a way that is both easily accessible and incredibly nuanced. They provide a developmental roadmap and the concrete tools we need to make partnerships work. In this book, I have finally found the resource I need."

Ethan Lowenstein, Associate Professor of Curriculum and Instruction
Eastern Michigan University
Ypsilanti, MI

"The approach of this book is fresh, current and multifaceted without being complicated. The authors have skillfully woven multiple and complex family and professional perspectives into a *well-integrated whole that is thoughtful, clear, and explicit. The material is relevant, useful, and extraordinarily helpful to a wide variety of dance partners."*

—Camille Catlett, Scientist
FPG Child Development Institute, University of North Carolina
Chapel Hill, NC

"This book comes from the heart of an author who knows both sides. The content is relevant, immediately useful, and encourages us to think deeply about ourselves and how we can apply the information to make a difference—all evidence-based components of effective adult learning."

—Juliann Woods, Professor Communication Science and Disorders
Director, Communication and Early Childhood Research and Practice Center
Florida State University
Tallahassee, FL

"The authors never forget that it is all about the children/students with disabilities—so the adults just need to figure it out! They include many subtle examples of how inclusion can work throughout the book. An important take-away message is that becoming true partners takes time and is a process."

—Peggy A. Gallagher, PhD, Professor of Early Childhood Special Education
Georgia State University
Atlanta, GA

"The authors help readers to understand that relationships are about human needs and feelings, not just about facts, and that partnerships only develop to their potential when each party can both share and listen to content and facts as well as the needs and feelings of the other. This book is destined to be a classic. Give it to someone you care about; and read it yourself reflectively."

—Michael Peterson, PhD, retired Professor and Director of
Whole Schooling Consortium (www.wholeschooling.net)
College of Education, Wayne State University
Detroit, Michigan

"The authors of this book offer a welcomed, kind, and needed message for both professionals and parents— slow the pace—stop and listen. The authors know we build each partnership one at a time. This is a message we desperately need to get into higher education and professional development communities."

—Mary Jane Brotherson, Professor
Iowa State University, Department of Human Development and Family Studies
Ames, Iowa

"This book reminds teachers and professionals to include parents in the timeline of the special education process. The information that parents contribute and different perspective they provide can help us understand the whole child. As I finished this book, I developed a more open perspective to working with parents."

—Maura Crown, Special Education Teacher, MS 3rd grade collaborative teaching model
Monroe, NY

"I found myself nodding in agreement with virtually all the points made in this book. The process is, indeed, a dance. Although one would think we have mastered dancing, each student, each family, each day brings forth a new dance. As partners and parents we need to tweak out that uniqueness in the child together."

—Jo-Anne Dobbins, Director of Pupil Personnel Services
New Paltz Central School District
New Paltz, NY

REVISED EDITION

Parents and Professionals
PARTNERING *for*
CHILDREN
WITH DISABILITIES

A Dance That Matters

Janice M. Fialka • Arlene K. Feldman • Karen C. Mikus
Foreword by Ann P. Turnbull

CORWIN
A SAGE Company

CORWIN
A SAGE Company

FOR INFORMATION:

Corwin
A SAGE Company
2455 Teller Road
Thousand Oaks, California 91320
(800) 233-9936
www.corwin.com

SAGE Publications Ltd.
1 Oliver's Yard
55 City Road
London EC1Y 1SP
United Kingdom

SAGE Publications India Pvt. Ltd.
B 1/I 1 Mohan Cooperative Industrial Area
Mathura Road, New Delhi 110 044
India

SAGE Publications Asia-Pacific Pte. Ltd.
3 Church Street
#10-04 Samsung Hub
Singapore 049483

Acquisitions Editor: Jessica Allan
Associate Editor: Allison Scott
Editorial Assistant: Lisa Whitney
Project Editor: Veronica Stapleton
Copy Editor: Dan Gordon
Typesetter: C&M Digitals (P) Ltd.
Proofreader: Dennis W. Webb
Cover Designer: Rose Storey
Permissions Editor: Karen Ehrmann

The stories in this book are based on the authors' experiences. Some of them represent actual people and circumstances. Individuals' names and identifying details have been changed to protect their identities. Other vignettes are composite accounts that do not represent the lives or experiences of specific individuals, and no implications should be inferred.

Cover Artwork: A Conversation with Katie by Candee Basford
This painting came to be after a conversation with my daughter Katie who taught me the importance of participating in the dance of community in order to reach our dreams.
Cover Quote 1 from *The Quantum Society: Mind, Physics, and a New Social Vision* by Danah Zohar and Ian Marshall
Cover Quote 2 from *Tempered Radicals: How People Use Difference to Inspire Change at Work* by Debra E. Meyerson

Interior art by Jen Boyak.

Funds for initial development of the material in this book were provided by the W. K. Kellogg Foundation, grant #P0034324.
Printed in the United States of America.

All trade names and trademarks recited, referenced, or reflected herein are the property of their respective owners who retain all rights thereto.

Printed in the United States of America.

Library of Congress Cataloging-in-Publication Data

Fialka, Janice.
Parents and professionals partnering for children with disabilities : a dance that matters / Janice M. Fialka, Arlene K. Feldman, Karen C. Mikus ; foreword by Ann P. Turnbull. — Rev. ed.

p. cm.
Rev. ed. of: Do you hear what I hear? : parents and professionals working together for children with special needs / Janice Fialka, Karen C. Mikus ; foreword by Ann Turnbull. c1999.
Includes bibliographical references.

ISBN 978-1-4129-6639-9 (pbk.)

1. Children with disabilities—Family relationships. 2. Developmentally disabled children—Family relationships. 3. Parents of children with disabilities. 4. Special education—Parent participation. 5. Children with disabilities—Services for. 6. Developmentally disabled children—Services for. I. Feldman, Arlene K. II. Mikus, Karen C. III. Fialka, Janice. Do you hear what I hear? IV. Title.

HQ773.6.F53 2012 305.9´084083—dc23 2011052015

This book is printed on acid-free paper.

Certified Chain of Custody
SUSTAINABLE FORESTRY INITIATIVE
Promoting Sustainable Forestry
www.sfiprogram.org
SFI-01268

SFI label applies to text stock

14 15 16 17 18 10 9 8 7 6 5 4 3

Contents

Foreword

It is a common experience across human nature that we like to receive gifts. Big gifts, little gifts, gifts of all kinds and varieties. In the spirit of the joy of experiencing gifts, I want to share my perspectives on two gifts that I treasure.

My first gift is Janice Fialka. Janice is truly a positive force in my life. I have had the good fortune of having Janice as a friend for a very long time. Sometimes I am in more frequent touch with her, and sometimes it may be months between our conversations. Regardless of the frequency of contact or lack thereof, every encounter that I have with Janice I can truly call a gift. I always learn, always laugh, and always feel a sense of solidarity that she is a reliable ally in our shared pursuit of making significant and sustainable enhancements in quality of life for individuals with disabilities and their families. Of Janice's many attributes, I especially appreciate her wisdom and nurturing ways.

I am reminded of the proverb that "a tree is known by its fruit." Janice has a truly amazing son, Micah Fialka-Feldman, who has "broken the glass ceiling" when it comes to students with intellectual disabilities attending college and pursuing national advocacy roles. I have had the good fortune of watching Micah's DVDs (www .throughthesamedoor.com) and benefiting from his own wise insights about his journey to an inclusive adult life. I applaud Micah's self-determination and vision in his accomplishments, but I also am well aware of the "partnership tree" that launched Micah into such a successful life. Janice is "known by her fruit."

Although I have not had the privilege of knowing Arlene Feldman and Karen Mikus, I know that if Janice chose to work with them, they share her values and proclivities or trusting partnerships with families. Thus, not only Janice but also Arlene and Karen are gifts not only to me but to you as well.

The second gift is this amazing book. *Parents and Professionals Partnering for Children With Disabilities: A Dance That Matters,* Revised, is transformational in its impact. Yes, it provides a solid basis of information, but it moves beyond information to enable us as readers to examine our immediate reactions to the challenges and opportunities of partnerships, our core beliefs that are tied to our immediate reactions, and our overall frame of reference of how we come to partnerships—whether we are a parent or professional. Thus, your encounter with this book will not just be a "quick read," but rather an opportunity for self-reflection of assumptions and feelings, identification of priorities for personal change, exploration of potential new ways of forming relationships, opportunity for building competence for new roles, and incorporation of new perspectives into every day actions. Truly, this is the essence of transformation.

Although I really was not aware that the first edition of their book had room for improvement, Janice, Arlene, and Karen have taken this revised edition to a new level with additional family vignettes from both family and professional perspectives as well as extensive new material on the building blocks of partnerships—especially in challenging situations, such as when parents are experiencing anger or appear to be "uninvolved" from the professional's perspective. This additional material is an added treasure in truly being able to act wisely.

I have every confidence that my two gifts—this author team and this book—will be received by you in a similar way. Consider yourself fortunate to have picked up this book. I can guarantee that you will consider yourself bestowed with partnership treasures when you have embraced the lessons that lie herein. This is indeed your lucky day. You might even consider it your birthday—a birth of new partnerships celebrated with your new gifts.

I encourage you to adhere to one of Janice's favorite admonitions—"the power of pause." This book is one in which you owe yourself the chance to pause, savor, and become transformed.

Ann P. Turnbull, Distinguished Professor
of Special Education
Beach Center on Disability
Department of Special Education, University of Kansas

Preface

When we (Janice and Karen) met in 1994, we quickly learned that we shared a passion for understanding parent-professional partnerships. From both personal and professional experiences, we knew that when partnerships between families and professionals worked well, everyone felt confident, empowered, and energized. A sense of enjoyment and fulfillment pervaded these relationships, and most importantly, the children with disabilities benefited with responsive, creative, and comprehensive interventions.

We also knew that when these partnerships were not working well, everyone felt drained, stiff, and waning in their sense of hope. Everyone dreaded meetings and wished that the relationship problems would just go away so that the focus could be about the child. To everyone's surprise, forming partnerships often felt more challenging than living with and teaching a child with disabilities. We spent many hours discussing what we had termed this "dance of partnership." As we dug deeper into the topic, we wanted to engage the broader community of parents and professionals to enhance our understanding of what skills, perspectives, and attitudes made partnerships work. How is trust developed? How is conflict successfully negotiated? How are relationships sustained when time and resources are limited? How do we encourage, nurture, and support positive relationships, especially given the emphasis on parent-professional partnerships in educational, health, and human service settings?

In 1995, the W. K. Kellogg Foundation awarded the Center for Human Development at William Beaumont Hospital in Michigan a grant that allowed us the time, energy, and resources to study parent-professional partnerships for one year. We were excited! We conducted a literature review; met with scores of caring, talented, and committed parents and professionals; participated in numerous trainings; and met weekly to discuss our evolving ideas and questions. We brought our voices and unique experiences as a parent of a child with disabilities (Janice) and a psychologist working with children and families (Karen) to each and every discussion. We learned more about our similarities and differences, and were humbly reminded that our different voices both challenged and enriched our partnership.

LEARNING FROM PARENTS, PROFESSIONALS, AND THE FIELD

With the support of the grant, we developed a daylong training on building effective parent-professional partnerships titled *The Dance of Partnership: Why Do My Feet Hurt?* and piloted it in Michigan, Iowa, and Indiana during the grant period. (Janice continues to facilitate this training as a workshop and keynote nationally to parents and professionals.) We set the expectation that whenever possible, the audiences should be comprised of both parents and professionals. We viewed this being "in the same room" as a very effective strategy to enhance the understanding of what parents and professionals uniquely experience.

Responses from the participants overwhelmingly confirmed what we hoped would occur as a result of these trainings—a better understanding of each other's perspective, a keener appreciation for the complexity of forming partnerships, enhanced empathy for each other's constraints and contributions, and an increased sense of hope that partnerships are indeed necessary and possible.

THE BEGINNING OF THE BOOK

In 1998, as a result of our study of partnerships and the valuable thoughts offered by the participants at our trainings, we compiled some of our writings on partnerships into what we called a "little book" inspired by our conversations, trainings, and investigation. The W. K. Kellogg Foundation graciously funded the printing of 1,000 copies of this collection, which we distributed, at no charge, to parents and professionals, mainly across Michigan. We never anticipated that this "little book about partnerships" with its long title, *Do You Hear What I Hear: Parents and Professionals Working With Children With Special Needs,* would go beyond the first printing in December 1999. Surprised and delighted, we received numerous requests for the book for use in professional development trainings, university and community college classes, family workshops, and for personal reflection by parents and professionals. A decade and eight additional printings later, *Do You Hear What I Hear?* continues to have relevance and significance for families, for new and veteran professionals, for the higher education community, and for professional development trainers.

When Corwin expressed interest in publishing the book with additional vignettes, essays, and strategies, we were thrilled. We invited Arlene Feldman to join us as an author and to contribute her valuable experiences and rich insights gleaned from her forty years as a general and special educator, a principal, a director of special education, and a college instructor. Her desire to pass the torch to new and future educators of students with disabilities, so that they may work hand in hand with the families of the children, has enhanced the depth and breadth of the book, and its relevancy to educators.

Acknowledgments

Thank you to the many parents and professionals from across the country who have shared their stories of becoming partners. You have inspired us with your honesty, tears, humor, creativity, passion, and incredible persistence.

We are grateful to the many people who reviewed the first drafts of our manuscript over ten years ago. Each of you offered meaningful and astute comments and heartfelt encouragement. In particular, we thank Martha Blue Banning, Lisa Ellis, Rich Feldman, Fran Loose, Linda Klenczar, Cindy Higgins, Ann P. Turnbull, Vicki Turbiville, Betsy Santelli, and Pam Winton. Carolyn McPherson skillfully edited many sections of the 1999 original manuscript and gave us the brilliant idea to portray the internal thoughts and feelings of parents and professionals through stories. This has been the anchor of our book.

A grant from the W. K. Kellogg Foundation and administrative support from the Center for Human Development of William Beaumont Hospital provided us with the rare gift of time to study and reflect upon parent-professional partnerships. We are grateful to Marvin McKinney of the W. K. Kellogg Foundation and Ernest Krug at Beaumont for supporting our work.

For this new and expanded version of the book, we enthusiastically add to this list of fine people to thank. We were graced with wise words and sound suggestions and enthusiastic "keep going!" cheers from: Susan Addison, Alice Audie Figueroa, Jennifer Champagne, Tamara Faggen, Harvey Feldman, Katie Feldman, Marla Feldman, Rich Feldman, Emma Fialka-Feldman, Micah Fialka-Feldman, Kathy Garrett, Jackie Gollinger, Aryn Kruse, Melissa Lesser, and Cindy J. Weigel. Each spent untold hours reading, thinking, eloquently sharing, and encouraging us.

The PEAK Parent Center and Linda Rowley shared their knowledge of first-rate resources for families and professionals.

Laurinda Phillips steadfastly answered the same formatting questions a million times, retyped a million pages, and lovingly said a million times, "How else can I help?"

Near the end of this writing, Jennifer Champagne and Susan Addison saved the day and got us unstuck. You both dazzled us with your clarity, swift direction, insightful suggestions, compassion, and belief in our work. Your expertise and wise words are rooted on page after page.

Michael Peterson and Michael Castleman, both prolific authors, graciously shared their knowledge and guidance about publishing, giving us the confidence to take the next steps.

Candee Bright's painting "We Dance Together" vividly graces the cover of our book. We are honored to have it be the first thing that readers see. Its gorgeous colors, sweeping movements, and hopeful spirit embody Candee's dynamism and her driving belief that we must find ways to work together to support the dreams of all people. We encourage readers to enjoy more of Candee's paintings (www.wedancetogether.com).

Jen Boyak's talented artistry and imagination moved the dancers from the cover to the inside pages. We are delighted that she could be a part of our project.

The Corwin staff, especially David Chao and Jessica G. Allan, gave new meaning to the word patience. Jessica did not give up on us, and we are most grateful.

There is absolutely no way that we would have completed this new edition without our talented editor, Kelly Boyle. She came to this dance with elegance, humor, honesty, and skill and brilliantly helped cut away the clutter. We are deeply indebted to her.

Thank you to all named and unnamed who guided us in our belief that the parent professional partnership *is* a dance that matters.

Janice M. Fialka
Arlene K. Feldman
Karen C. Mikus

ADDITIONAL ACKNOWLEDGMENTS FROM JANICE

I want to thank my colleagues (families and professionals) across the country, including those at Clinton County RESA's

Early On Training and Technical Assistance project who courageously and constantly demonstrate what it takes to "keep dancing." I have learned so much from each of you. Thank you to Christy Callahan who gave me the needed support and time to hide away in my basement office to write, and to Meg McSweeney and Carolyn Sinai who pulled me out of the basement and into the light just when I needed it. I have immense gratitude for my coauthors, Arlene Feldman and Karen Mikus, for being willing to join me on the dance floor. There is no solo dancing.

I am indebted to Elizabeth Bauer, Sharon Berke, Mary Jane Brotherson, B. Kay Campbell, Camille Catlett, Shirley Chalmers, Mel Clayton, Marsha Forest, Kae Halonen, Lisa Houghtelin, Norm Kunc, Sharon Luckerman, Cynthia P. May, Carly Murdy, Patty McGill Smith, Shaun Nethercott, Jack Pearpoint, Mary Pipher, Judith Snow, Beth Swedeen, Ann P. Turnbull, Emma Van der Klift, my many women friends, and my Busy Women's Reading Group for supporting my writing and deepening my thinking. Each one of you made me stretch in new ways, even when I resisted learning the "hard stuff." I am truly blessed with an amazing village! My son, Micah, led me to the disability activist community, and I haven't been the same since! Through so many strong disabled activists, especially Naomi Ortiz, Sarah Triano, and the staff of the National Youth Leadership Network, I have learned about disability pride and culture and have been inspired to understand my journey in new and more enlightened ways.

Katie Kramer's steadfast and passionate belief in this book kept it afloat during ambiguous times. Since our first conversation, I have been touched by her compassion to partner with families and her zeal for the book.

Thank you to Holly Sasso who led me to Kelly Boyle, and who has encouraged my writing over the years in ways that have had a profound impact on my life.

Susan Addison has helped me see what I couldn't see and coached me to dance my dream for years. I can't imagine my life or poems without you.

My parents, Al and Dolores Fialka, and my siblings, Gerry, Nancy, and John, have sustained me and taught me to dance to all of life's music with joy at my feet. My sister, Nancy, a veteran teacher, has shown me what great teachers can do with humor and dedication.

Our children, Micah and Emma, continuously teach us new dance steps, and though we stumble a lot, they lift us up over and over and have confidence that we can learn new dances. I can never thank my husband, Rich Feldman, enough, though I will never stop trying. You are my favorite dance partner!

ADDITIONAL ACKNOWLEDGMENTS FROM ARLENE

First and foremost, I would like to thank Janice Fialka for inviting me to coauthor and provide the educator's perspective to the second edition of this book. Our mutual respect and admiration for each other's passion, experience, and success, and our ability to share and meld our individual perspectives, have, for us, created a strong and meaningful partnership of parent and professional!

Next, I would like to thank Jo-Anne Dobbins, Carol Washington, Patty Kennedy, and Michelle Thompson, the dedicated and hard-working women who worked with me in the Special Education office of the Valley Central School District. For many years, they read my reports, brochures, prospective presentations, articles, and so on and told me over and over again that when I retire, I should consider writing! Thank you for planting that seed!

I'd also like to thank my wonderful friends for their ongoing support of my endeavors during this journey. With a twinkle in their eyes, they'd ask teasingly, "Are you still working on that book?" I would especially like to thank my good friend Tamara Fagen for her editorial expertise.

Those same thanks go to my brother, George Karp, my sisters-in-law, Rita and Kathy, and most of all to my mother-in-law, Pearl Feldman, a retired teacher, who has always been my role model! I know that my dear parents, Estelle and Jack Karp, would be so proud of my accomplishments.

I can never thank my children enough—Jackie and Brad, Matt, Melissa and Kevin, Andrew and Katie—for their ears, their questions, their thoughtful comments, and their belief in me! Thank you to Jordan, Dakota, Maya, Ethan, Mac, Jackson, and Madison, my adorable grandchildren, for making me realize that you are the beneficiaries of the partnership between your parents and your teachers!

Finally, I would like to thank my wonderful husband, Harvey Feldman, for just about everything! As a developmental optometrist, for over forty years, he has been providing vision therapy to children and working collaboratively with their parents to ensure the provision of follow-up exercises at home. He personifies the concept of the parent-professional partnership. He has been my inspiration throughout my professional career and will always be the apple of my eye!

ADDITIONAL ACKNOWLEDGMENTS FROM KAREN

I would again like to thank the parents, children, and professionals with whom I have had the privilege to work for several decades. They have shared their stories of struggles and triumphs and helped me understand the nuances of partnership from so many perspectives. Their journeys comprise truly incredible stories and valuable lessons.

My Uncle Dick (Richard S. Clark of Butler, Pennsylvania) continues to inspire and amaze me. He has lived graciously and courageously with a variety of disabilities (cognitive, language, motor) for 89 years.

He was institutionalized at the age of 5 after my grandmother could find no community program for him. He never received any education or therapy. Throughout my childhood and teen years, we visited him several times a year and shared parts of his world on those visits. It was eye-opening for me and deeply shaped my decision to become a special educator and then a clinical psychologist. He was deinstitutionalized at the age of 55 and gloried in living independently for the next 20 years. He has made special friends of the staff and other residents at the personal care home where he now resides.

He continues to chortle when he teases me and delights in beating me at dominoes. Most importantly, he is one of the most emotionally astute people in my life. He never fails to ask me about whatever family or emotional issue is at the forefront of my life. For ten years after his sister (my mother) died, he called me every month on her death date and we would share a moment of remembering her with love. I cannot thank you, Uncle Dick, enough for all you have taught me.

PUBLISHER'S ACKNOWLEDGMENTS

Corwin wishes to acknowledge the following peer reviewers for their editorial insight and guidance.

Renee Bernhardt
Ed.S Curriculum and Instruction
Cherokee County School District
Canton, GA

Dawne Dragonetti
Special Education Teacher
Nashoba Regional School District
Stow, MA

Esther Eacho
Education Specialist
Associate Faculty Johns Hopkins University
*   School of Education, Special Education*
Baltimore, MD

Judy B. Engelhard, Assistant Dean
Emeritus Professor of Special Education
Spadoni College of Education
Coastal Carolina University
Conway, SC

Nicole Guyon
SPED Teacher
Providence Dept.
Cranston, RI

About the Authors

Photo ©2011 by Wendy Martin Photography

Janice M. Fialka, LMSW, ACSW, is a nationally recognized speaker, author, and social worker with an expertise in adolescent health, parent-professional partnerships, inclusion, and postsecondary education for students with intellectual disabilities. She has co-founded and directed several teen health centers in Michigan, and has previously taught at Wayne State University in the School of Social Work. She is the Special Projects Trainer for Michigan's *Early On* (Part C of IDEA) Training and Technical Assistance. Over the past two decades, Janice has provided the keynote address and conducted workshops at numerous national and international conferences for audiences of families, school personnel, educators, social workers, early interventionists, health care providers, and community groups. Janice serves on numerous national advisory boards and has received several awards for her advocacy work, including 2007 Social Worker of the Year by National Association of Social Workers (NASW)-Michigan Chapter.

Janice and her husband, Rich Feldman, coproduced an award-winning DVD, *Through the Same Door: Inclusion Includes College,* which was given the 2006 TASH Image Award for the Positive Portrayals of People With Disabilities. This film documents their son, Micah's experiences as a college student. Micah, a rising leader in the disability movement, is part of the new wave of young adults with intellectual disabilities who continue their learning on a university campus.

Janice has coauthored three books, numerous articles, and a CD of several of her poems, entitled *From Puddles to PRIDE: A mother's poems about her son, his disability, and her family's transformation* which includes her often-published poem, "Advice to Professionals Who Must Conference Cases." Her website, www. danceofpartnership.com, is a highly regarded comprehensive resource for parents and professionals. In 2009, Janice and her family received the Family Voices Lifetime Achievement Award in Washington DC for their work in advocacy and disability.

Janice and her husband live in Michigan and are the proud parents of two adult children, Micah and Emma. They have had the joy of presenting as a family in their keynote address, "How Micah Grew His Beard, and Other Family Stories of Growth." Janice can be reached at janice.fialka@gmail.com, follow her on Twitter@JaniceFialka, or friend her on Facebook. Additional information at www.danceofpartnership.com and www.through thesamedoor.com.

 **Arlene K. Feldman**, MA, PD, SDA, LDT/C, began her career in education in 1967, at the ripe old age of 20. The depth and breadth of her experience within the field is varied and extensive. She has been in education for over 40 years, serving as a general education teacher, a special education teacher, principal of a special education preschool, and, for more than 20 years, a director of special education. Arlene is currently an adjunct professor at the State University of New York at New Paltz. Her greatest educational accomplishment, for which she was presented the Excellence in Leadership Award by the New York State Council for Exceptional Children, was the introduction and development of the collaborative teaching model (co-teaching within the inclusive classroom) in her school district. Believing in the benefits of collaboration, she is also passionate about the partnership between professionals and parents of students with disabilities. She fervently strives to inspire her graduate students, the next generation of educators, to welcome students with disabilities into their inclusive classrooms, understand their strengths and challenges, meet their unique needs, and enable them to succeed. She advocates working

earnestly and collaboratively with parents for the benefit of the students.

Arlene and her husband, Dr. Harvey Feldman, a developmental optometrist, live in New York and are the proud parents of four and the proud grandparents of seven with two on the way—and, hopefully, more to come! Arlene can be reached at arlene.k.feldman @gmail.com.

Karen C. Mikus, MEd, PhD, feels privileged to have been working with families of children with special needs and related professionals since 1970. She has a background in special education and is a practicing clinical psychologist. She has been a practitioner and/or an administrator in a variety of settings including school systems, hospitals, and mental health organizations. A frequent speaker and trainer for both parents and professionals, she also consults with preschools and schools regarding children's development and behavior. Drawing on her experience running social skills groups for young children, she enjoys training and supervising play coaches to facilitate interaction between children with social challenges. Previously, Dr. Mikus taught the course, *Working With Families of Children With Special Needs,* in the School of Social Work at the University of Michigan.

Introduction

Let us put our minds together and see what life we can make for our children.

—Chief Sitting Bull

*P*arents and Professionals Partnering for Children With Disabilities: A Dance That Matters is written for both parents and professionals, new or seasoned and is intended

- to demonstrate the absolute necessity of building strong and compassionate partnerships between parents and professionals;
- to identify and strengthen the skills needed to form and maintain effective partnerships;
- to analyze the complexity of these partnerships; and
- to inspire a renewed spirit to build and sustain strong parent-professional partnerships.

As we had dared to hope, the first edition of this book found its way into institutions and families, for it is our premise that the dance requires both parents and professionals. It has become a standard text for many higher education courses in a wide array of university and college departments. The range of courses includes assessment, family systems, collaboration strategies, consultation, working with families, education, and intervention taught in departments as diverse as early childhood, education, family and child development, nursing, pediatric residencies, psychology, social work, special education, and the various specialized therapies such as audiology, occupational therapy, physical therapy, and speech-language therapy.

School districts have provided the first edition for entire staffs who have read it for personnel development and for in-service trainings. It has been placed on bookshelves and used in reading groups at many family resource libraries and parent centers. Parents have given it to professionals and professionals have given it to parents in an attempt to help the other dancer hear their music. And, perhaps most important, the book has found its place on the desks and bedside stands of parents and professionals who feel stuck in their partnership and are urgently seeking ways to get back on the dance floor so that the children will soar.

In this revised edition, we have incorporated many suggestions from a variety of readers: both parents and professionals. The reader will find additional scenarios, more practical tips, updated resources, and in-depth discussions of the complexity of building and maintaining partnerships in the 21st century.

HOW THIS BOOK IS ORGANIZED

In the first chapter, The Dance Toward Partnership, we present ways to think about partnerships using the metaphor of "the dance" to illustrate key concepts about this unique working relationship between parents and professionals. In many ways, learning to partner is similar to learning to dance together. Initially, toes get stepped on as partners try to find common rhythms and shared dance steps. We propose a developmental approach to understanding relationships. Forming partnerships is a process. It is not instant or automatic, but rather evolves and changes over time. We explore how partnerships meander through and around three phases, each with definite characteristics. Real-world vignettes involving parents and professionals illustrate each of the three phases, from "Colliding and Campaigning" to "Cooperating and Compromising" and finally to "Creative Partnering and Collaborating." Practical suggestions for parents and professionals about ways to help partnerships become more productive and compassionate are included.

Chapter 2, Listening to the Hidden Lyrics: Tuning in to Your Partner, contains two stories told in several scenes from the perspective of both the parent and the professional. In the Story of

Sam (also found in the original edition), we highlight the experiences of a psychologist and a mother whose 4-year-old son is going through the assessment process. The Story of Rachel takes place at four pertinent points in the special education process in an elementary school. In both stories, we take the reader below the surface of what is typically said between parents and professionals, and listen to the "hidden lyrics," the internal feelings and thoughts of both the parent and professional. Practical suggestions are provided throughout the stories.

In Chapter 3, The Dance Manual: Essential Steps to Keep on Dancing, two comprehensive lists of straightforward, ready-to-use strategies and insights to maintain the relationship are presented for both parents and professionals. These go-to lists can be reviewed during any phase of the partnership: before, during, after, or upon reflection.

In the fourth chapter, When the Dance Is Complicated, we delve deeper into two situations in which parents are labeled— mislabeled—as either angry or uninvolved. A different and more sensitive perspective of these complicated dances is revealed. We suggest a way to reframe these troubling interactions in hopes that a new way of listening will inspire us to take off our judge's wig, unfold our arms, lean forward, and listen more intently to our partners with a new heightened sensitivity.

In the fifth chapter, Enhancing the Dance: Partnership Notes, we explore the benefits of exchanging notes or what we call "partnership notes." Over the years, we've learned that when parents and professionals share positive and practical feedback with each other in the form of verbal communication and written notes, relationships are strengthened and deepened. We also present various modes of communication used by professionals to keep families abreast and aware of their child's learning as well as class and school activities.

In our concluding thoughts, we reiterate why the parent professional partnership *is* "a dance that matters," emphasizing the importance of trust, time, and listening.

A WORD ABOUT WORDS USED IN THE BOOK

In the book, we use the term "parent" as an inclusive term to mean *any* person who primarily supports the child and who is viewed as being in the "parenting role."

We also use the word "professional" as an inclusive term to mean any person who supports the learning of the child, such as a teacher, a home visitor, an administrator, a paraprofessional, an early interventionist, a therapist from a variety of fields, and so on.

We use the term "disability" as an inclusive term to mean *any* developmental delay, any physical, cognitive, or emotional disability, and any, what the field has called, special needs or special education label.

In this book, we primarily use "people-first language" (e.g., "person with a disability"). This format is preferred by many because it supports the idea that people should be thought of as a person first instead of having the label be identified first.

We also respectfully recognize that many people in the disability community prefer "identity-first or disability-pride language" (e.g., "disabled person"). The thinking behind this format is that disability is not a bad thing and that it should be embraced as an essential part of one's identity—a natural part of humanity. (For a deeper discussion on language, see *Reap What You Sow: Harvesting Support Systems,* an excellent curriculum for disabled youth and their adult allies developed by the National Youth Leadership Network [www.nyln.org].)

Words matter, but what really matters is our commitment to engage in conversations with each other about our beliefs and values. Ultimately we know that no label can ever truly capture the unique magic, potential, and gifts of a child. That is why knowing and using individual names is really the most preferred "label" to use.

To watch us dance is to hear our hearts speak.
—Hopi saying

The Dance Toward Partnership

Using the Dance Metaphor to Understand Parent–Professional Partnerships

Forming partnerships between parents of children with disabilities and the professionals who work with them is like learning a new dance. At first, the parent dancer and the professional dancer do not glide together gracefully across the floor. Their moves are likely to feel stiff, uncertain, and awkward. The partners may have different expectations, needs, and constraints. Each seems to be listening to his or her own music, with its own tune, words, and rhythm: there's the child's song, the mother's song, the father's song, the teacher's song, the special educator's song, the administrator's song, the therapist's song, the physician's song—no shortage of music! No wonder some partnerships are not as graceful as others; the absence of shared music and familiar dance steps causes collisions. Toes—and feelings—get stepped on (Fialka, 2001).

Forming effective partnerships between parents and professionals requires that partners take time to listen to their own song and each other's song. This kind of listening has the potential to open the partners to a fresh approach and a broader perspective on what the child needs. As parents and professionals share their insights, worries, dreams, and suggestions with each other, a new song—a new plan—is created, one that contains the contributions of many voices. This new plan weaves together several perspectives. It's no longer just "your" swing dance or "my" salsa. It's an original musical score with new choreography based on the unique needs and gifts of each child.

No one person can "dance the dance" or create the best program for and with the child. The best plans are built upon the insights, perspectives, and expertise of both parents and professionals, eventually with the full participation of the child as she or he grows. It takes teamwork—and a complex choreography in which the synergy of the dancers creates the most comprehensive and effective supports and interventions for the child.

This dance of partnership, easy to describe on paper, is far from easy to achieve in reality. Partners will not always be graceful, and few get it right on the first tries. Master dancers achieve success through practice and skilled coaching. The performers on *Dancing With the Stars* do not spin, twirl, and whisk each other across the floor on the first take. They practice, persist, and listen to each other as well as their coaches. They bump into each other with impatience and frustration. They worry about how they might be judged by the onlookers. Eventually, if they are going to make it to the finals, they learn to trust each other and to share the same rhythm—or at least complement each other's unique rhythms. Ultimately, theirs is a dance that awes and inspires audiences.

The dance image can be useful to parents and professionals in guiding their understanding of partnerships formed on behalf of children.

To sit at the conference table together and discuss the child with disabilities is an essential beginning, but it does not automatically result in a genuine partnership. We may look like partners but not *be* partners—yet!

The best dance results from a strong, ongoing commitment by all partners to listen to each other's music, try out each other's dance steps, and trust that a new dance will be created, one that integrates the most creative contributions of each partner.

At the forefront of this work, we must remember that parents and professionals must set aside their egos and work together on behalf of the child. The reward for a well-performed dance of partnership comes from knowing that the child has been given the support needed to reach his or her fullest potential—rooted in the highest of expectations. That accomplishment—the evolving and ultimate ability of the child to dance his or her unique dance—is sweet music to everyone's ears!

HOW THE DANCE BEGINS

There is no escaping it these days. Partnership is a recurrent buzzword in the fields of education, health, and human services. "We must be partners. Collaboration is the name of the game." This is the message of administrators, policy makers, professionals, and parents. Articles, posters, and textbooks echo this refrain.

Partnership is indeed a worthy cause, one that appears easy to believe in and own. However, effective partnerships can be elusive, hard to grasp. "So—is this a partnership?" "What's it supposed to look like?" "Why is it so hard?"

After reading and thinking about parent-professional partnerships for several years, we realized that the frustration sometimes felt by parents and professionals is often due to misunderstandings about the nature and evolution of partnerships. For example, there is often the expectation that parents and professionals become partners the moment they sit down at a conference table to discuss plans and goals for a child. Our experience has been just the opposite: Partnerships evolve over time and go through a series of developmental phases during the course of working together. It is our intent to describe the phases parents and professionals cycle through as they form and maintain effective partnerships.

It Takes Time

Before we explore parent-professional partnerships using this developmental model, it is important to understand the social-cultural context in which these relationships exist. We live in a society seduced by immediate gratification—a fast-food mentality. What began with instant burgers and instant coffee now includes instant messaging, instant banking, instant information—all of which feed our expectation that things can (and should) happen *now. Right away! This second or sooner!*

But not all processes can be shortened and accelerated. There is virtually no way around the fact that relationships take time. They develop through conversations, problem-solving, listening, and overall hard work—all fundamental to creating trust. There is, in fact, no magic for speeding up the process of forming a solid working partnership.

Nor can we expect smooth sailing and effortless perfection along the way. Instead, we must realize that we will have to work slowly and carefully to become true partners; that we will make mistakes and experience setbacks; that we will learn to make repairs; and that we will need large reserves of patience, forgiveness, hope, and trust in order to forge effective and durable relationships that benefit our children.

We believe that a developmental approach to partnerships is both realistic and useful. Such an approach suggests to us that there are identifiable phases with tasks that must be completed before partners are able to move to the next level. This way of thinking helps us to view challenges and struggles in our relationships as normal and inevitable, rather than as hopeless indicators of a doomed relationship.

Frustrating or challenging as these interactions may be, they can be understood as a "typical" part of the process of working together. Being out of sync sometimes *is* part of the dance. In the words of the visionary author Margaret Wheatley (2009), "We expect it to be messy at times."

Do I Wanna Dance?

As we hope you can see, the dance metaphor is a particularly useful one for understanding partnership. However, even before two people get on the dance floor together, a litany of questions emerges—questions that float, invisible and unspoken, in search of answers that don't come easily or quickly. Therefore, it is important to contemplate these unexpressed preliminary questions, because they capture the anxiety and hesitancy that naturally frame the dance toward partnership.

The first question often asked is, "Do I even want to be at this meeting, at this dance?" For parents in particular, the partnership with professionals is not a chosen relationship. Most parents did not plan to be involved in special education or special services, so although parents might need the support, guidance, or knowledge of the professionals, they often feel hesitant about stepping into this new and unsought relationship. Thus at the outset, the partnership is a dance of ambivalence: "I need you in my life, but I don't always want you in my life."

Professionals, on the other hand, typically feel eager to share their expertise, resources, and skills. "Let's begin this dance. I am ready! I have much to share with you."

When their enthusiasm is met with hesitation, folded arms, or other signs of parental disengagement, professionals may feel frustrated, even hurt. Quietly they may be thinking, "I'm only trying to be helpful!"

My Reflection: What can be done or said to ease this awkwardness, ambivalence, or initial uncertainty?

Seasoned professionals offer the following advice when encountering a hesitant parent: "Don't take it personally! In most situations, the reluctance to connect is not about you, the professional, but rather about the life-changing circumstances forced onto the family. It's important to remember that most parents didn't choose to be at this dance."

With time and support, families move onto the dance floor having choreographed their own dance based on their family's values, preferences, and strengths—based on *their* music! Families grow, adjust, and thrive in their own ways and in their own time. It is up to the professionals to get to know each family and to honor each family's unique ways of coping, shaping their lives and supporting their children.

Professionals, too, may experience elements of an unchosen quality to their dance. Most professionals chose to work with children and rightly feel that their primary partner is the child. Yet professionals soon learn that along with the child comes another set of partners—the parents, who bring another set of important issues, expectations, and desires. Moreover, in many situations, professionals, early in their careers, may have limited training, experience, and guidance working with families. Having the parents as part of the team comes as a challenge, sometimes even as a surprise. Professionals may ponder, "Wait . . . you mean I have to dance with *you* too! How do I do that? What do I know about *your* music?"

Increasingly, because of the mounting expectations to "do more, with less," providers are feeling the squeeze of too many partners on the dance floor. Nowadays, it is common to hear providers whisper behind closed doors, "I love my work, but I don't know how I am going to handle so many children, families, forms, requirements, and meetings."

Thus both parents and professionals often begin this working alliance with a certain reluctance or ambivalence—not an easy way to begin.

In addition to asking "do I wanna dance?" other common questions may linger back stage.

- What if I am ready to dance hard and fast when you want a slow, gentle dance?
- If I follow your lead, where will you take me? Will you follow my lead?

- What if we collide, trip, or fall? Will we be able to pick ourselves up and continue dancing?
- Can I set aside my experiences with previous partnerships and truly begin this new one with a clean sheet of music?
- And for those who have already been dancing strenuously on behalf of their children or students, a quiet question, born of exhaustion: How much energy do I have to begin another partnership?

These are basic but important questions. Ignoring them can complicate the partnership process; being sensitive and open to them can heighten the possibility of a rich beginning.

My Recollection: If I remember only one thing from my reading about the parent-professional partnership and the dance metaphor, it is

PHASES OF THE PARTNERSHIP DANCE

A Cautious Beginning to the Dance

When parents meet with professionals for the first time, they are likely to feel out of place. Everything is unfamiliar: the faces, the titles, the little chairs, the language, the forms, the procedures . . . the overall experience.

Even veteran special education teachers who unexpectedly become parents of a child with a disability will attest to how awkward they feel at their first meeting as a parent. Despite their years of knowledge and expertise, they report a strong sense of vulnerability and even helplessness.

Professionals, too, may feel uncomfortable encountering parents for the first time. What will this family be like? Easy to engage? Reluctant? Quiet? Withdrawn? Trusting? Emotional? Hard to read?

In many ways, this initial meeting is like a middle school dance. There is self-consciousness, uncertainty, and an absence of trust. Like young teens at their first dance, potential partners eye each other cautiously, wondering who should make the first move.

My Reflection: What can professionals and parents do and say to acknowledge and ease some of the awkwardness of these initial meetings?

Phase 1:

Colliding and Campaigning

Despite the awkwardness that new partners are likely to feel, the time will come when they are face to face on the dance floor and the music begins. The dance is under way. Unfamiliar with each other's rhythms, moves, and styles, these new partners will not be in synch right from the start. Instead, they're likely to stumble, lurch in opposite directions, and even collide.

For experienced partners who have learned to trust and understand each other, a little collision along the way is no big deal. It's a cue to pay closer attention, and by carefully communicating with each other, they can quickly recover and continue on with their dance.

For new partners who lack a depth of experience and common understanding, an initial collision or conflict, no matter how small, can shut off the fragile connection that has begun. In an effort to restart the communication, or at least to make themselves be heard, parents and professionals frequently move into a "campaigning" phase.

During this phase, both partners strongly articulate their own perspectives in hopes of persuading the other to see the child, the problem, or the intervention similarly. Much like politicians during an election year, each campaigner carries his or her sign with space enough for only one viewpoint. It is the very nature of campaigning to cleverly and powerfully put forth one's idea. Dialogue is not part of the process.

Partners come to this dance with deeply rooted values and perspectives that have been developed over decades, even generations. Opinions on solutions, interventions, or next steps are fiercely held, and the ideas or approaches of the other may seem unfamiliar or contradictory. People often jockey for power, protect territory, block the other's solutions, and try to sell a particular position. Although these behaviors seem negative and difficult, such campaigning is actually a positive reflection of the partners' strength of commitment to the child or the program. The problem is, "campaigning" partners are not working together. They are dancing solo . . . and solo dancing ultimately and dangerously limits how a child learns and grows.

> **My Reflection:** Think about a time in your own personal life when you felt strongly about a situation. Describe the circumstances. What did you want to have happen? What was underlying that desire—what values, dreams, past history, and expectations? What did you want the other person to understand about your perspective?

The Language of Colliding and Campaigning

In this phase of the partnership, we frequently hear language like this: "I really want it done this way." "This is the way it works." "That's not how we do things here." "That wouldn't work." "I really know what's best."

Hope and possibility are easily swamped when campaigning prevails.

Imagine the Dance of Colliding and Campaigning: The Story of Josie

Jim and Donna Lopez are parents of a blended family that includes Donna's teenage son, Jim's 9-year-old daughter, and their daughter together, Josie, age 6. Josie, who was born with moderate cognitive impairments, loves animals, art, all the Disney princesses,

and "going to school." This past year, Josie went to a special education preschool-kindergarten, where she received speech and language therapy, occupational therapy, and physical therapy within
the classroom setting. As the school year came to a close, Josie's
annual review meeting was scheduled to review her progress and to
determine services and supports for the upcoming year.

Jim and Donna Lopez arrived at the meeting with mixed emotions. They felt some anxiety because their little girl would soon be
leaving the cozy environment she had come to know so well. On the
other hand, they were excited about Josie starting first grade at
Jefferson Elementary, the neighborhood school their older children
had attended and where Donna herself had gone 30 years ago.

The meeting began on a cordial note as the parents, teachers,
and therapists shared their observations of Josie's progress over
the past year. Josie's teacher remarked on her improving verbal
skills, and the occupational therapist reported that Josie was making strides with writing and using scissors. Mr. and Mrs. Lopez
noted that Josie, despite her stubborn moments of "I won't," was
overall happy and helpful at home, often putting her toys and
clothes away with only a little bit of nudging.

The meeting was off to a good start, until the discussion
turned to plans for Josie's next school year.

Ellen Watkins, the school psychologist, smiled at Mr. and
Mrs. Lopez and reiterated how pleased the team was with Josie's
progress this year. She expressed their confidence that Josie would
continue to excel next year in the school district's Opportunity
Room, a special education class recently moved to the new school
"just a short bus ride" from the Lopez home. The class was taught
by Anna Tseng, a seasoned special education teacher highly
regarded for her ability to create a nurturing classroom.

Josie's current teacher enthusiastically chimed in, "Oh, you'll
love Miss Tseng! She has the same high expectations for students
as I do, and we know that's important to you. Miss Tseng is also a
master teacher with the new reading program—perfect for Josie."

This enthusiasm was met with pained looks and a stunned
silence from Mr. and Mrs. Lopez. The staff was baffled by the parents' reaction. They had taken great care in making their recommendation and genuinely wanted the best for Josie.

"But . . ." Donna glanced at her husband for support, "we
want Josie in the *regular* first-grade classroom, maybe even with

Mrs. Todd." Mrs. Todd had taught both of their older children—and perhaps now it was Josie's turn. Moreover, Josie's parents had rigorously researched educational options for their daughter. They began to see how Josie would and could excel in their neighborhood school, with the right supports, just as their other two children had.

Ms. Watkins was quick to sympathize. "Yes, it must be hard to envision a different experience for your daughter. But we've considered it carefully. We feel that Josie is not quite ready for a full general education experience yet. We believe that students with cognitive impairments integrate better *after* they've spent the initial couple of years in a more specialized program . . . getting ready."

"But . . . we've thought a lot about this. I know some other people—" Mrs. Lopez faltered on, "my cousin's son in Florida has Down syndrome, and he was included all the way through school. We know it works . . . it's what is best for Josie."

"But that's not been our experience," said Ms. Watkins. "And Josie will get lots of opportunities to be with typical students, as she'll be with them during art and gym classes. The special education classroom at Sutton School is the best environment for your daughter right now. She'll be in a supportive, nurturing classroom with a specially trained teacher . . ."

"In a separate school and in separate classroom. . . . To us, that's segregation!" exclaimed Mr. Lopez, his face red with emotion. "You just said that Josie was doing well . . . we want her in the regular classroom with support and with our neighbors' children."

What had begun as a friendly meeting rapidly deteriorated as parents and professionals volleyed back and forth—getting more entrenched, getting more demanding, getting nowhere. It was as if the Lopezes were waving a sign that said "Do Not Segregate Our Daughter" and the professionals were waving a sign that said "The Special Education Classroom Is Best." At that moment, neither side felt they could put down their sign and listen to the other. Both sides were campaigning, with the best intentions, but still without any movement.

Still stuck in their positions after almost an hour of fruitless debate, the parents and professionals in Josie's annual review meeting finally agreed on something: they needed a new approach to plan for Josie's next school year.

My Reflection: Describe three feelings that the parents are experiencing and three feelings that the professionals are experiencing. Identify some of the interests and values influencing or shaping the two different opinions about where Josie should be next year—from both the parents' and the professionals' perspectives.

Moving Forward: Dance Steps to Practice

STOP: It's impossible to learn new steps while you're still dancing the old. So pause, breathe deeply, find a place of patience. Modulate your voice to a conversational tone so you can move away from the dance of debate and toward the dance of discussion.

LOOK: Step outside yourself for a moment. What would an impartial observer see and hear? Observe and describe what's happening. Acknowledge that there is a difference of opinion and articulate it. "OK, it seems that we don't exactly agree right now. Let's take some time to identify our different perspectives." Don't pretend or gloss over the differences.

LISTEN: In order to dance smoothly together, partners must get to know each other. Especially if they've gotten off on the wrong foot, now's the time to be curious, not furious. Being curious requires dropping the defenses, leaning forward, and asking for more information.

Resist the impulse to debate. This does not mean abandoning your position; it merely means setting it aside for the moment so you can hear what your partner has to say. Remember, this step is all about listening. Similar points of view and possibilities for compromise are more likely to surface when partners feel heard and respected.

"Tell me more about what you are thinking" is an important follow-up prompt, as it encourages the others to share the hopes and worries they may not articulate at first.

Remember that listening does not imply agreement. Rather, it implies a commitment to learn more about the other's point of view.

SHARE: Identify the important values, feelings, and goals that emerge during the deep listening. It's likely that you will find some common ground to build on as you prepare to step back out on the dance floor. Typically, when we are at the standstill phase of "campaigning" we share what is at the "tip of the iceberg." In other words, we share what we want to happen in this situation. In order to get unstuck, our conversation needs to focus on what are the unspoken concerns and deeply held values influencing what we want. In order to get unstuck, we have to explore what's behind our thinking, what's below the surface. This level of conversation is the only way to get unstuck . . . but it takes patience, trust, and a willingness to listen and share. Have no illusions, listening during times of disagreement or differences is exceptionally hard to do. It can't be rushed, and may require that not all the dancers meet together at the same time. Patience and good coaching are needed.

TAKE CARE: Resist rushing to solutions and dashing to decisions. Make sure you understand your partners' goals and perspectives— it can be helpful to write down their main interests for all to see and review. Even experienced partners collide and fall, so return to the listening phase often.

Sometimes it's important to postpone the conversation or bring in someone else to partner, such as another school professional skilled in negotiation or who has some prior positive rapport with the family or child. An outside mediator who can assist or facilitate the discussion is another alternative. These options need not be seen as signs of failure, but rather as creative steps in working toward resolution in challenging times.

Unfortunately, some relationships never move beyond this first phase of hammering away at separate agendas. But if people do agree, even momentarily, to take time to explore what's below the surface, they are less likely to remain glued to their separate positions. Small new insights might be realized. New dance steps might be tried. Trust might begin to emerge, and the dancers might find ways to compromise or at least quiet the noise of campaigning.

My Reflection: Now that you've reviewed the list of possible next "dance steps," take 10 minutes to write a dialogue—a conversation between the parent and the school psychologist. Free-write what each might say. Follow up with one suggestion you'd make to both the parent and professional for the next steps in working through this impasse.

My Recollection: If I remember only one thing from my reading about the phase of "Colliding and Campaigning," it is

Phase 2:

Cooperating and Compromising

During the middle phase, partners continue to feel some apprehension and uncertainty but are also likely to feel more of a balance and some hope. As trust emerges, so does a spirit of cooperation. There is an expectation of working together to explore and ultimately arrive upon next steps, programs, and services that best meet the needs of the child. As a result . . . there are fewer collisions, less stepping on toes. An important ingredient to this middle phase is that partners are reliable—they follow through on agreed upon tasks, and if they can't, they inform the other of their constraints and continue to look for solutions.

How did the partners move out of the campaigning and into the more rewarding phase of cooperation and compromising? The small and fragile trust born in the first phase is strengthened when the partners agree to work side by side without insisting that "my way is the only way." Compromises can be arranged so that each person feels that crucial goals for the child are being addressed.

At this level, people are more effective in their listening. They are more likely to use the phrase, "Tell me more about what you think." There are more attempts to genuinely consider the other person's ideas, hopes, dreams, and expectations, or at least be able to acknowledge them. In part, these newer and more welcomed ways of interacting occur because partners are getting to know each other. Each feels an emerging sense of respect for the other and begins to believe in the effectiveness of their joint problem solving. There is a sense of moving in a similar direction and of matching each other's dance steps.

The Language of Polite Cooperation

The language that often characterizes middle-phase parents and professionals is the language of polite cooperation: "You do your part and I'll do mine." "Maybe that will work. Let's try your idea." "Tell me more about what you're hoping for, so that we can incorporate it into the goals."

Fortunately, at this phase, people are more apt to listen and ask about others' ideas, with genuine curiosity in their voice and heart! They are more able to suspend—not necessarily abandon—their personal agendas and explore common ideas and areas of potential agreement.

Working together at this level often generates effective supports for children and a sense of satisfaction for partners. Parents and professionals have told us that most relationships remain at this phase and are less likely to move toward Phase Three, primarily because of time constraints for both families and professionals.

This phase should not be dismissed or viewed as a bad place to be. On the contrary, relationships at this phase have cooperation and reliability at their core. Trust is developing as commitments are honored, problem solving is practiced, shared meanings are emerging, and some level of consensus is expected.

Imagine the Dance of Cooperating and Compromising: The Story of Andrew

Mr. and Mrs. Bashid have three children. Their twin daughters are in third grade, and 5-year-old Andrew is in kindergarten. Like his older sisters, Andrew was a happy and precocious baby, walking and saying several words even before his first birthday. But things suddenly changed just after he turned 2. He stopped talking and playing with his beloved squeaky ball. He stared into space. He no longer seemed happy. The Bashids felt as if the Andrew they loved had suddenly disappeared.

Their family pediatrician suggested that Andrew be evaluated, resulting in a diagnosis of autism. Stunned and devastated, the Bashids withdrew from many family gatherings and community activities. Although they had heard the word "autism," they had no experience with this label or with special education services. Secretly, they worried that Andrew's autism might be a result of something they had done.

The initial meetings with the school staff were tense and overwhelming for Mr. and Mrs. Bashid. They had immigrated to this country five years earlier and considered themselves bilingual, yet much of this special education language left them confused and annoyed.

Several times, Mr. Bashid raised his voice saying, "You must stop talking about my son as if he is stupid." The special education staff wondered if Andrew's father understood their words. "That's not what we are saying, Mr. Bashid. We didn't say he cannot learn. We know he can. Please understand that we are here to help." Over the coming weeks, Mr. Bashid grew impatient with this phrase, which to him seemed patronizing. Inside he fumed, "Does it look like I need your help?"

During this first year of special education services in elementary school, colliding and campaigning were a part of most meetings between the Bashids and the special education team. Discussions were fraught with tension and misunderstanding, and neither parents nor professionals felt they were being heard. Trust and cooperation seemed almost unattainable; it wasn't a good year.

The next year, before school began, Andrew's first-grade teacher, Ms. Tenak, invited the Bashids to meet with her before "all those official meetings where everyone seems so serious!" In her phone call to the Bashids, she did her best to sound welcoming. "I'm looking forward to having Andrew in my class. Over the years, I've learned that parents have so much to teach me about their children. I'm hoping that we can meet, and you can tell me about Andrew. What's he interested in? How does he learn best? What does he like to do at home?"

With some reluctance, Mr. and Mrs. Bashid agreed to meet. As they nervously entered the classroom, Ms. Tenak thanked them for coming, offered tea, and apologized for having to squeeze into the child-size desks. She smiled and took a deep breath. "I want to know about Andrew—through your eyes."

Though hesitant at first, Mr. and Mrs. Bashid slowly opened up about Andrew—his fear of dogs, his interest in cars, and his fascination with Legos. They broke into hearty laughter when Ms. Tenak shuffled through a folder of papers from last year and showed a class photo of the dress-up party, featuring Andrew as a huge red Lego. Mr. Bashid proudly pointed to his wife. "It was Mrs. Bashid's idea. She knows Andrew loves his Legos."

At Ms. Tenak's request, Mr. and Mrs. Bashid shared more stories about Andrew. They felt a welcome sense of connection developing with this teacher who took such an interest in their son, even spending time reviewing his last year's work. As the meeting drew to a close, Ms. Tenak asked if they had any particular concerns. Mrs. Bashid was silent and looked to her husband. Mr. Bashid said, "My son can learn. Do you understand that?"

Tension flooded back into the room, and Ms. Tenak resisted the impulse to respond defensively—to wave a sign that said "You're not listening to me!" Instead, she consciously balanced herself and replied, "It sounds like you have some concerns. Are there things that are troubling you? What's important for me to know?"

After a few comments were shared, Ms. Tenak indicated that they didn't have to solve every problem at this first meeting. "Let's continue to talk and find other ways to communicate with each other," she said. "What works best for you?"

Mrs. Bashid softly sighed. Mr. Bashid simply said, "I like seeing photos of Andrew, and I like telling stories about my son." Ms. Tenak nodded, "That's a good start. I'm sure we'll have many more photos and stories to share." In spite of the slow beginning and a few tense moments, all three left the meeting with some positive feelings about working together.

Although the rapport developed during that first meeting went a long way toward establishing a good working relationship, challenges did arise. Halfway through the year, Ms. Tenak heard about a new program that provided socialization between students with autism and fifth-grade "buddies" as they worked on computer-based lessons. She felt that this afterschool experience would be beneficial for Andrew, and was frustrated when the Bashids did not respond to her two phone calls or the note she sent home.

Just when Ms. Tenak was about to give up on the afterschool buddy idea, she saw Mrs. Bashid in the school hallway. Both teacher and mother offered stiff hellos and barely made eye contact. Ms. Tenak asked, "I'm wondering if you got my phone . . ." Interrupting, Mrs. Bashid said, "I am sorry . . . we didn't call. It's . . . just that we . . . we don't . . . think that special program is right for our son. He knows about computers; he's good with computers. We don't want him to stay at the school so long."

Ms. Tenak tried to hide her disappointment, "I am glad we're talking, Mrs. Bashid. I think this would be such a great help to Andrew. Could we give it a try for one month?"

Although the Bashids were firmly against an afterschool program, they were beginning to trust Ms. Tenak's judgment and wanted to cooperate as best they could with her recommendations for Andrew. After discussing the issue several times, teacher and parents eventually reached a compromise: Andrew would have a fifth-grade buddy twice a week during reading time, just like several of his classmates already did. It wasn't the program Ms. Tenak had in mind, but it provided Andrew with extra socialization without setting him apart or keeping him after school.

The year was marked with a feeling of growing trust, and although neither the Bashids nor Ms. Tenak felt as if they had the perfect parent-teacher relationship, it was what they called "good enough." Most importantly, it was a good year for Andrew.

According to Mr. Bashid, "Most of the time the meetings were helpful, especially seeing all the new photos of Andrew in class. The teacher tried some things that didn't make a lot of sense to us, and she tried some things that we wanted, too. As my grandfather use to say, 'a little bit here and a little bit there.' One thing I know for certain: It's a lot better than the first year when I didn't feel I could trust anyone, including myself."

Moving Forward: Dance Steps to Practice

STOP: It's easy to fall into the trap of labeling the partners in the dance as either "the parent" or "the professional." When we stop this categorical thinking, we discover that we share a common label. We are all people—each with our own stories, foibles, strengths, interests, and hopes. Casual conversations in the hallways, over the phone, or before and after meetings create opportunities to get to know each other a little bit better. We learn that one of us likes hockey, or enjoys gardening, or works the midnight shift. We may not become best friends or perfect partners, but moving beyond our labels into friendly interactions can enhance and strengthen partnerships.

LOOK: Look for opportunities to follow through on commitments you've made, big or small. Being dependable is a powerful way to build trust. Notify your partner when you anticipate a delay, a change in your agreement, an unexpected barrier, or when you have more ideas. If you begin to feel ambivalent about the agreed-upon plans, share your concerns or questions. Keeping silent will inevitably lead to misunderstandings. As suggested in the phase "colliding and campaigning," continue to be curious about each other's ideas, and look for common ground.

Look to others to talk through the challenges or to seek guidance. Trusted colleagues, family members, and friends can be helpful sounding boards, providing both validation for your feelings and brand-new insights. Stay away from people who encourage blaming or attacking others. That type of negative advice puts a screeching halt to building partnerships.

LISTEN: Listening is the most fundamental and probably the most challenging of all dance steps and must be constantly employed. Work on sharpening your listening skills throughout the dance. Listen for understanding and check in frequently to be certain you're on the same page. During conversations, reflect back on what you heard the other person saying. Ask if you got it right. Listen to your own chatter inside your head. Sometimes that chatter interferes with your ability to be truly open to someone else's thoughts.

Listen for the times when communication feels awkward or tense. Don't dismiss it or pretend it doesn't exist. There's a reason for the uneasiness. Paying attention can promote communication. Listen for when differences emerge, acknowledge the different perspectives, and explore the range of opinions.

SHARE: Notice what is working well in the partnership. Let your partners know what has been productive, what you appreciated, and what was helpful. Feedback like this has a reinforcing impact. Partners are more likely to keep doing what worked when it is acknowledged. Most of us second-guess ourselves, at least occasionally. Receiving appreciation and specific feedback bolsters confidence and energizes partners and the relationship as a whole.

It's also important to share when unusual stresses or life changes, such as a family illness or an unexpected deadline, might impact interactions or the partnership. Details aren't necessary, but a heads-up can help explain changes in the routines or even how communication is handled.

Some parents experience an unexpected and increased sensitivity at significant anniversaries, birthdays, or other predictable times such as at the annual review meetings or during what some parents call the "I.E.P. (Individualized Education Plan) season." Being aware of these possibilities enhances the team's ability to be sensitive, kind, and understanding.

> Don't forget to review the dance steps from Colliding & Campaigning—We never outgrow our need to keep practicing the basics!

TAKE CARE: When we stumble on each other's toes, apologies go a long way to repairing and strengthening the partnership. An honest "I'm sorry" is a natural part of all healthy relationships. Take care and work toward a shared meaning of the vision for the child and for how "success" is defined.

My Recollection: If I remember only one thing from my reading about Cooperating and Compromising, it is

---

Phase 3:

Creative Partnering and Collaborating

Inquiry and listening continue to be the cornerstones of successful alliances at this level just as they were at the earlier levels.

Third-phase partners tend to share their interests, needs, fears, worries, and hopes with one another fairly readily and openly. They are more apt to talk about what is below the surface, what really matters. The security that comes from knowing that one's hopes, dreams, goals, and concerns are truly important to and valued by one's partner enables a kind of exploration and problem solving that results in brand-new solutions and fresh ideas for intervention. No longer are partners dancing separately; nor are there two distinct dance lines as we often see in the middle phase. Instead, the music and the choreography are now original works composed by all the partners. Together the partners have written goals and strategies that result from many ideas, not "yours" or "mine," but rather ours. As the child gets older, she or he becomes an integral partner and, with support, authentically participates and ultimately leads, to the extent possible, the discussions, planning, meetings, and future visioning.

Partners at this third level typically see the child in a similar way and share common expectations for him or her. When situations are viewed differently, which still happens, partners are open to exploring and understanding the differences. At this third level of creative partnering, the child is central to the dance. He or she is in the middle, the focus, the reason for the partnership.

During this phase, partners do not feel the need to "tell and sell" their solutions; rather they believe that innovative and totally new solutions are possible and probable if they explore ideas and work together. When conflict or differences in opinion are present, they are not viewed as threatening. Stomachs don't churn and faces don't flush quite as easily as they do in the earlier phases. Conflict during this phase is acknowledged as a normal part of partnering and viewed as an opportunity to really work on the "important issues" to ensure that the child reaches his or her potential. Partners know that they will get a clearer understanding of everyone's concerns and hopes as they explore the conflict and differing views of the issue. Challenges still occur, but instead of ignoring or glossing over the bumps, partners at this level acknowledge their part and offer the necessary "repairs" with care and compassion. "I'm sorry" or "I regret" are valued and understood to be part of the working partnership.

Power and decision-making tend to be balanced. Interventions become blended, integrated, and unique.

The Language of Possibility

The language often heard in this phase is the language of creative opportunity and possibility, which sounds like: "Let's see what we can create together." "I think 'ours' is better than 'mine' or 'yours.' " "I've been worried about this program for my child. I want to talk about it with you. Maybe we can create something different. What do you think? I could really use your ideas about how to handle this situation."

Creative partners experience a sense of promise and hope, as well as feelings of efficacy and satisfaction. Their solutions are far from perfect but can be adjusted and refined in order to assure the most appropriate setting, supports, and interventions for the child.

This is the phase in the relationship that genuinely feels safe, satisfying, creative, and most productive.

Imagine the Dance of Creative Partnering and Collaborating: The Story of Tyrell

When her adult daughter, a single parent, was killed in an automobile accident eight years ago, Bernice Ruby was left to raise her two grandchildren, Keisha, then 8, and Tyrell, then 3. Although Keisha was never sick, Tyrell, who had been a colicky baby, was plagued with bouts of diarrhea, stomach spasms, eczema, asthma, and hives. After countless examinations, the pediatrician referred Tyrell to an allergist to determine if these ongoing medical issues were allergy-related. Not surprisingly, tests indicated that Tyrell was allergic to peanuts, tree nuts, eggs, dairy, pollen, mold, and dust. His allergies were severe and potentially life-threatening.

Frightened by this serious diagnosis, Mrs. Ruby was determined to protect her grandson while keeping him as typical as possible. On the pediatrician's advice, she received early intervention services in her home. Tyrell went on to receive services as a preschooler and then as an elementary school student. Over time, and with lots of work on the part of his family, Tyrell learned which foods were "Tyrell-friendly" and which were not allowed. He knew that anyone playing with him needed to wash his or her hands first, and he tried his best at alerting an adult immediately if he "felt 'sick-y' or breathed funny." Coaching Tyrell over the years to help him understand his needs and having a few well-informed adults nearby resulted in a childhood remarkably unscathed by serious health disasters.

When Tyrell entered kindergarten, Mrs. Ruby was extremely anxious about her grandson's welfare. So many children, so many interactions, so many dangers! But she quickly found the school staff to be understanding and willing to make adjustments to ensure Tyrell's safety. Together, Mrs. Ruby and the school professionals crafted a plan to protect Tyrell from allergens throughout his school day. The school agreed to these measures:

- Designate Tyrell's classroom and his lunch table in the cafeteria as peanut-free zones.
- Provide a paraprofessional to wipe Tyrell's desk and lunch table, to make sure he eats only "Tyrell-friendly" foods, and to watch for signs of breathing problems.
- Provide EpiPen training to Tyrell's teachers and paraprofessional.
- Provide wipes to each classmate to be used after lunch and recess.

As allergies had always been a part of his life, most of the time Tyrell accepted these precautions matter-of-factly, and his six years at the elementary school went by with no major health incidents—a relief to everyone! Even the few close calls and everyone's willingness to discuss what could be learned from these near-slips helped build trust and confidence in the team's efforts to maintain a safe environment for Tyrell.

Tyrell participated in Little League and Boy Scouts and played the drums in the school band. There were days when Tyrell seemed irritated by all the fuss at lunch time. There were a few times the staff had to search for Tyrell when he didn't appear in the cafeteria for lunch. But more days than not, he seemed to accept the routines established at school.

Now things were about to change: Tyrell would be entering middle school in the fall. His upcoming annual review meeting was extremely important since a new group of professionals would be learning about him, and together with Tyrell, his grandmother, and the elementary school team, designing a program at the middle school that would address his unique health needs.

Mrs. Ruby was anxious. The more she thought about Tyrell in middle school, the less she slept. His new school was huge—it seemed larger than the new shopping outlet. No matter how many staff members kept their eyes on Tyrell, she knew he couldn't and probably shouldn't be "watched" all the time. What if the student sitting next to him had an egg for breakfast or peanut butter for lunch? The elementary school staff, students, and parents had understood the seriousness of the situation. Would the middle school staff be as vigilant, understanding, and compassionate?

Sheila Brown, the director of special education, was also anxious about this meeting. She had invited several of the elementary school staff along with key staff from the middle school to participate. She knew that the strong relationship between Mrs. Ruby and the elementary school was the result of years of ongoing honest conversations, continuously making adjustments, and problem-solving between home and school. Her goal for today's meeting was to make sure that an equally strong partnership be created, or at least initiated, with the middle school staff.

The large elementary school music room was used as a conference room to accommodate everyone. Mrs. Brown greeted the large group as her eyes circled through each of the 24 people sitting around the table, including Tyrell and two of his classmates. "We certainly are a village!" she chuckled. "I want to welcome all of you and share what we've learned as a team since Tyrell began his first year here as a kindergartner. We have a list of our 'lessons learned' to review with you. But before we share these, I want to get a little bit philosophical with you. I hope you don't mind." She paused and waited for a few heads to nod.

"When our team started this journey with Tyrell and his family six years ago, frankly we were worried, maybe even scared at times. The 'what if's' hung over us like ominous rain clouds. At the time, I was reading Peter Senge and his work about learning organizations. Inspired by his wisdom, I discussed with my staff one of his main points: 'Begin with the end in mind.' This simple phrase reinforced for me how important it was for teams to create a shared vision as a guide to their day-to-day practices." A few of the staff nodded as they recalled those earlier days.

Mrs. Brown continued, "Six years ago, as we sat at this same large table, I encouraged our team to begin with a shared vision about Tyrell's future. I asked Mrs. Ruby what she wanted to happen for Tyrell during his years in our elementary school. I can still hear what you said, Mrs. Ruby. Do you remember?"

Mrs. Ruby nodded, "Of course I do . . . I said, 'I want my grandson to be safe *and* be a *regular* kid in his school.' "

"Yes, Mrs. Ruby. Exactly! Your words focused us. It may sound a bit simple, but this vision has guided us in our planning every single day. We hope it helps you—his new team at the middle school." For a moment, the room filled with an unfamiliar still-ness, not typical of the music room.

Mrs. Brown took a deep breath, smiled at Tyrell, and said, "It's your turn, Tyrell!" Tyrell jumped up and with his two classmates raced to the AV cart, announcing with pride, "We made an awe-some PowerPoint called 'Welcome to Tyrell's World.'" With confi-dence and humor, they told stories of how they learned about "Tyrell-friendly foods" and the importance of frequent hand washing. They showed cleverly captioned photos of Tyrell and friends proudly displaying their blue ribbons at a science fair, hanging out in the band room, and goofing off at recess. It was abundantly clear that Tyrell was, indeed, a "regular kid" at school.

Tyrell's principal, school nurse, teachers, and therapists went on to describe his program, his strengths, needs, and interests. As they spoke of the many accommodations that were currently being provided, Mrs. Ruby nodded gratefully, wiped her tearful eyes, and voiced her thanks to the team that had worked with her to keep Tyrell safe and healthy for all these years. Mrs. Brown reminded everyone that the success they saw at this meeting didn't just happen. "We want to stress that our ability to work together was a result of numerous conversations and problem-solving moments. It's been done here, and it can be done at the middle school. We want you all to continue our work to keep Tyrell out of harm's way."

Ms. Trice, the director of food services at the middle school, took a deep breath and stated, "Well, I can't say I don't have some concerns, but if the elementary school can do it, so can we. We will designate a peanut-free area in the middle school cafeteria where Tyrell can eat and be with his friends." She indicated that she would also review all food items and remove those containing nuts. Looking directly at Tyrell, she said, "OK, young man, we're going to make some changes to keep you safe. But we'll need your help too. Don't think we can do this all by ourselves."

Tyrell rolled his eyes, "Sure . . . I've heard that before."

Mrs. Ruby liked how the staff talked directly to Tyrell, and she was relieved that the cafeteria would now be a safer place for her grandson. She felt even better when Mrs. Brown said, "Let's talk about all the other things we do for Tyrell here and see how we can do the same at the middle school."

The nurse said she would be happy to teach the sixth-grade teachers how to use the EpiPen and emphasized that she would be on call if an emergency arose. The school custodian promised to order wipes for all of the students in each of Tyrell's classes. Mrs. Ruby was reassured that Tyrell's paraprofessional would be accompanying him to the middle school, but here she spoke up. "This is a big concern for Tyrell," she said. "We have to work on not letting her hover over him. She's excellent at supporting Tyrell, but if his new friends see Tyrell coming down the hall with a 'mother' attached to him, they'll avoid him like the plague." Tyrell's two friends confirmed, "You got that right!" The new principal noted that he'd place this issue at the top of the discussion list.

The school bell sounded, announcing the end of the school day. For Tyrell and his buddies, the meeting was over. They gathered their supplies and hurried off to band practice.

Uncertainty still hovered over every adult in the room, but Mrs. Ruby felt the stirrings of hope replacing the dread she'd carried for the past several weeks. She and Mrs. Brown shared a smile, both believing that this new team was starting on the right foot. A new dance was beginning, and the partners left the meeting with feelings of resolution, commitment, and hope—and as to be expected, a few worries too.

Staying Put at Creative Partnering: Dance Steps to Practice

STOP: Periodically stop and reflect on how trust was achieved in this partnership. What did it take? What challenges did the team face? How were compromises reached? Remember what it took to arrive at this phase of creative partnering and collaboration. Spend a few minutes at an annual review meeting to stop and acknowledge the strategies practiced by the team. Keep a written list to share with future teams.

LOOK: Look to the future and anticipate what new partnerships will be formed as the child moves forward in his or her schooling. Intentionally plan how the team will make a smooth transition to new partnerships. Allow for time to express feelings that come with saying "good-bye" to partners with whom you've worked.

LISTEN: Teams never outgrow their need to listen to each other. Even at this advanced phase of partnership—when trust is enduring and the foundation is strong—listening is as important as it was at the very first meeting. As the child grows, remember to encourage and support the child's genuine participation in meetings and planning.

SHARE: Share what supports, interventions, and activities have been effective. Keep a list that can be given to new partners or new programs. Remember that the only constant partner for the child is his or her family. Professional partners, though important, will come and go. It is only the family who is most likely to remain at this dance with the child. Support families to be strong and effective advocates by sharing the knowledge, resources, and strategies discovered over the years.

TAKE CARE: Take time for self-care. Families and professionals have enormous demands pulling at them in numerous directions. Ask yourself, "What do I need to do to restore my energy and refresh my perspective?" Taking care of ourselves is not a "nice thing to do when there is time." It is as necessary as the air we breathe! Having a hobby, regular exercise, reflection time, recreational or spiritual activities—whatever provides enjoyment and rest—is as important as a well-written I.E.P.

> Remember to review the dance steps in the previous phases.

My Recollection: If I remember only one thing from my reading about Creative Partnering and Collaborating, it is

Caveats and Suggestions

As in all developmental models, no one moves through these three phases in a clear, predictable, and ascending manner. We move up and down, back and forth, get stuck, skip stages, repeat and revisit former phases. Circumstances can cause us to move erratically in our relationships. For example, a new diagnosis, a transition to a new school or services, a change in personnel, and family stressors for either the parents or the professionals can all have an impact on our ability to partner. Each child, family, and team of professionals has a unique way of interacting and moving toward the phase of creative partnering. There is no one right dance—no one way for all partnerships.

We have also learned from many parents and professionals that few working relationships get to the third level of creative partnering. Think about it. Most of us have only a few people throughout our lives with whom we can feel that unwavering sense of trust. The third phase of partnership as described here takes time, conversation, courage, and a strong belief that working on the relationship is worth it, in the short run and long run.

Each of these three phases is rooted in real events and expectations. We gain insight as we better understand our current position in these phases. If we know where we are, we can explore how we got there and what we can do to move forward.

We will not be able to dance gracefully with everyone, in every situation, every year. Sometimes we have to ask others to do the dancing for us or with us when we are at a standstill with a particular partner. Maybe the teacher consultant or other staff member might partner more easily with a particular teacher, rather than having the parent immediately intervene. This type of mediation need not be seen as a failure, but rather as a creative way to deal with personalities that may clash or with circumstances that need more time or a brand new approach.

What seems important is that we all pay attention to the relationship and not discount or underestimate its significance in creating and achieving meaningful supports, plans, and programs for our children. In our partnership trainings, we suggest that the first goal of every plan, every Individualized Family Services Plan (IFSP), Individualized Education Plan (IEP), or any other service plan should be "to strengthen the parent-professional partnership." When we suggest this, members of the audience often smile in amusement, but begin nodding their heads in agreement. "Yes, that makes sense." When we genuinely function as a team, the plan we map out is more attainable, and success for the child comes closer to fruition.

Practical Suggestions

- As you begin a new relationship, think about the dance metaphor and the three phases that comprise the dance of partnership:

  Phase 1: Colliding and Campaigning

  Phase 2: Cooperating and Compromising

  Phase 3: Creative Partnering and Collaborating

- Remember that not all partners dance through these phases in a clear, predictable, ascending manner. Circumstances may cause partners to move up and down, return to former phases, or leap ahead.
- Remember that relationships need time to develop. Conversation, problem-solving, and hard work are required. Remember that smack dab in the middle of the word, col*labor*ation is the word *labor*. Indeed, partnerships take work!
- Remember the importance of listening in establishing and nurturing a partnership. "Listening allows you to demonstrate precise understanding of what another has said, and helps you be perceived as being competent and a worthy collaborator" (Friend & Cook, 2010).
- Rely on the insights, perspectives, and expertise of your partner, as both parents and professionals have much to offer.

 ## MORE RESOURCES

Harvard Family Research Project
http://www.hfrp.org/family-involvement/publications-resources

A Student's Guide to the IEP—National Information Center for Children and Youth with Disabilities
http://nichcy.org/wp-content/uploads/docs/st1.pdf

Special Quest: Multi Media Training Library
http://eclkc.ohs.acf.hhs.gov/hslc/tta-system/teaching/
Disabilities/Staff%20Support%20and%20Supervision/
Orientation/specialquest-training-library/specialquest-
multimedia-training-library.html

CHAPTER TWO

Listening to the Hidden Lyrics

Tuning in to Your Partner

The "dance of partnership" is an adventure laden with important experiences, realizations, and emotions for parents and professionals alike. All too often, however, these feelings, concerns, and hopes remain unarticulated and unaddressed—they are the hidden lyrics of the dance music. The power of unspoken worries and reactions should not be underestimated because they shape relationships and determine outcomes for the children involved.

Therefore, if partners can become more aware and sensitive to these needs and emotions, some of the stress and misunderstandings generated in partnerships can be reduced. Collaboration on behalf of children could then be that much more effective and enduring.

It is in this spirit that we offer the following two stories to illustrate a range of internal feelings and thoughts of both parents and professionals. Obviously, not all experiences will be the same for all partners. Our stories illustrate only some of the hidden lyrics of some parents and some professionals. However, the universality in the stories is the message that there is always a range of feelings, experiences, desires, worries, self-doubts, and expectations influencing our thoughts and actions. Relationships compel us to take time to consider what might be below the surface. This tuning in to ourselves and to our partners enhances our ability to be better partners—better dancers![1]

THE STORY OF SAM

The Situation

John and Susan Lewis have one child, Sam, who is 4 years old. Sam is an engaging and active child who has developed differently and more slowly than many of his peers. Some of Sam's delays are worrisome to his parents. John and Susan have taken Sam to several physicians and other professionals who have conducted numerous assessments of his strengths and needs. Most recently, Sam has been referred to the school psychologist, Dr. Rhonda Gordon, for a complete assessment in preparation for a kindergarten placement.

---

[1] The focus of this book is primarily early childhood and elementary school settings, when the primary partnership is between parents and professionals. These two voices are reflected in these stories. To experience the internal voice of a young adult with disabilities, the authors encourage readers to refer to *Whose life is it anyway? How one teenager, her parents, and her teacher view the transition process for a young adult with disabilities.* (Fialka, Mock, & Neugart, 2005)

Our Story's Design

These six scenes describe six moments in the lives of John and Susan Lewis, their child, Sam, and Dr. Gordon. The scenes take place before, during, and after Sam's initial assessment by the school psychologist.

Each of the six scenes is presented from two perspectives: first, the mother's, and then the professional's. After each scene, two lists of practical suggestions and considerations are offered: one list contains suggestions for professionals to consider from the parent perspective, and the second list contains suggestions for the parents to consider from the professional perspective.

SCENE 1

The Parent's Hidden Lyrics

John, Sam, and I have been ushered into your office. I had no idea there was an additional wing to our neighborhood school. But I never thought my child might need special education services, either. Sam is clutching his pride and joy, his new red train engine. He sings out "Choo-choo" as you greet us.

Since before his birth, we've had wonderful dreams for our son. We bring you our dreams, our doubts, and our fears. Why is he different? What should we be doing?

We've been through so much these last two years. First, our pediatrician said, "Everything is going to be fine. Sam's just a bit slower. He'll catch up." We tried to believe him, but after a few months and not much "catch up," I took him to another pediatrician. She wasn't as confident that his delays were typical. She led us to a neurologist, a geneticist, an audiologist, a speech therapist, more and more tests, and now to you, the school psychologist. It was hard to pick up the phone to make this appointment—you have no idea how hard. Just filling out your paperwork took more strength than I thought I had. Stepping over your threshold was an act of pure will. For us, everything we've wanted and hoped for is on the line. I wonder if you know that.

Our feelings are mixed. I find myself chanting: "Do well . . . don't do well. . . . Do well . . . don't do well. . . ." Part of me hopes my son will let you see all his difficulties and delays so you can get him more help. Part of me hopes that you will see all his strengths and abilities so we won't need any more tests, any more specialists.

Please know this. I'm not sure I can handle one more person telling me my child isn't "normal." I'm scared. At times, my husband and I feel lost, alone. I wish that all this worry would go away so I could go on being Sam's mom, being me.

The Professional's Hidden Lyrics

As you enter my office, I am struck by your faces: your child, beaming with pride as he shows me his toy train, and you, Mr. and Mrs. Lewis, your faces stamped with hope, fear, and grief. Week after week, families like yours come to me with their expectations and dreams.

Some parents are angry. Some appear withdrawn. Some are easy to talk with; others are more reticent. Some question my expertise—what makes me think I know what is best for their child? I'm wondering which way you will react.

You may not believe this, but this is difficult for me. You want me to fix it. Probably I cannot.

Your questions are complicated. You need answers and deservedly so. "Exactly what's going on with my child?" You will ask. "Why did this happen?" "What causes this?" "Will he be able to go to regular kindergarten or high school or college?" "Could he get married?" "What kind of job could he have?" "Which treatment is best?"

I long to give you answers, but often I just don't have all the answers.

The questions I must ask may evoke strong feelings in you. I know you have been to many other specialists. You must be tired of telling your story over and over. I will try to be sensitive to your feelings.

Are you desperate to hear the words "typical," "age-appropriate," and "everything will be fine"? What if I cannot say those words to you? What if the words I say are devastating?

I want to give you answers, but I worry they won't be the ones you want. I want to be helpful, to offer my knowledge, skills, and experiences, but I worry that, at least for now, it won't seem like help.

Some days, I feel very alone in this work.

A Few Ideas From the Parent Perspective

- I want your help, really I do, but I'd rather not *need* your help. I didn't choose my child's problems. Most days I wish the problems, the meetings, the tests, the worries would just go away. I just want to be Mom.
- I'm not mad at you. I'm tired and I'm scared. And I've seen so many professionals.
- I need your kindness.
- Help me know what other parents feel and think when they go through this.
- Please show me that you know this is tough.

A Few Ideas From the Professional Perspective

- Coming in to have your child tested must be very hard to do. Each parent comes with unique worries, questions, and knowledge. It helps me to know what would be helpful to you. I want to know your concerns and questions so I can be more sensitive and responsive. I will respect your thoughts and be careful with your feelings.
- Provide me with complete information about your child, including previous evaluations and interventions. Let me know if you agreed or disagreed with the findings.
- Let me know the conditions under which you are coming in for this evaluation. Did you choose to get this assessment, or were you pressured by another professional, by the school system, or by a family member?

NOTES

SCENE 2

The Parent's Hidden Lyrics

We sit down on your gray padded chairs. The sunlight behind you blinds my vision of you and your desk, so I push back my chair.

Sam, my Sam, wanders over to your bookshelf. I know he's looking for books about trains and trucks. Should I tell him to sit down? Or is it OK for him to roam? Which looks better in your eyes?

I'm anxious these days. Is this the sixth or seventh test? I've lost count, but I know there have been too many. Testing days make me even more anxious. I'm full of doubt and self-blame. How much of Sam's problem is my fault? My husband's? These days we argue more. Is that the reason for Sam's differences?

You seem to approve of Sam's roving. Smiling, you ask, "What do you like to read about, Sam?" My shoulders loosen. I relax a bit in my chair.

Now you explain about the tests you'll administer. I get stuck on the word "administer" and only hear bits of the next few sentences. Sam doesn't want to be "administered to." He just wants to play with his train.

"Any questions?" you ask. I wish I were armed with smart, impressive questions, but I just say, "Not yet." We reluctantly rise from our chairs and you point John and me toward the waiting room. I want desperately to tell you: Sam often needs to have questions repeated several times. Sam likes to play hide-and-seek. Sam hates hard chairs. Sam—there's so much I want to say. John looks stiff, but he thanks you and asks you how long the testing will take. I glue on my smile and say brightly, "Bye, Sam. See you later!" Sam smiles, waves good-bye, and then goes on playing.

I wonder if you have the answers.

The Professional's Hidden Lyrics

Your child has found my bookshelf and is flipping through the children's books I have collected over the years. I am drawn to him and want to join him in his search for train books, but I see your faces, Mr. and Mrs. Lewis, and instead I decide to address your uncertainties and questions.

I explain the tests I will use. Your shoulders stiffen, Mr. Lewis. You, Mrs. Lewis, rise from your chair and walk over to your child. You wrap him in your arms, pulling him ever-so-slightly away from me, as if you are shielding him.

Do I look so terrifying? Do my words, meant to comfort, do the opposite? I recall the first time I met with a family during my graduate internship. I was unprepared for the mother's flood of tears as I relayed the test results about her 4-year-old son who was diagnosed with autism. She taught me what no textbook could: how painful and frightening this process can be for parents. I have not forgotten that lesson.

I want you to know that I will look at your child's problems, but I will still see the wonder of him. I know he is special. You help me know just how special when you tell me about his favorite games, what makes him laugh, what you love to do together, as well as what challenges him and your family. I want to see Sam through your eyes, know the Sam that you know.

It is in your faces. You are afraid. You think your dreams for him are not safe with me. I feel some anxiety too. What am I going to see? What am I going to learn about your child that you know and wish were not so?

A Few Ideas From the Parent Perspective

- I'm a good parent. I want you to know that. Please ask what I think. I know so much about my child, more than anyone else in the world. I may not be able to describe him in the same words you use. Let me know that my words are just fine.
- Some days, evaluations and assessments feel like judgments of me as a parent.
- This is all new to me. Please tell me what to expect from your words, reports, and tests. Sometimes I don't know what the "next steps" will be. I can't always remember all the names of the professionals and tests. You can help by giving me written lists of the professionals' names, roles, and brief descriptions of the tests.
- If you tell me about my child's strengths as well as his challenges, I'll know you're seeing my whole child.
- Give me a chance to ask questions now and later. I may also need to ask the same questions over and over.

A Few Ideas From the Professional Perspective

- Tell me what you hope I'll see about your child.
- Feel free to ask questions now and later. I know this experience might be new for you. Sometimes parents hesitate to ask questions, especially in the beginning. I hope you'll be comfortable enough to share your uncertainties with me—at any point in time.
- I try to be careful and sensitive about the words I use. Forgive me if I use some that might offend you or that might not feel quite right. Let me know that, too. I am learning what is comfortable and acceptable for you and your family.
- One of the tough parts of my work is that I often have tight deadlines and a heavy workload. I will give you and your child every possible attention.
- Please know that I do this work because I want the best for your child.

NOTES

SCENE 3

The Parent's Hidden Lyrics

Two hours have passed. Finally, you and Sam come to meet us in the waiting room. He proudly pushes his train stickers too close to my eyes so I won't miss your gift. I glance at you, try to read your thoughts. I'm relieved you can't read mine. My desperation scares me.

You say you enjoyed meeting the three of us. "Sam worked hard," you say. You crouch down to Sam's level and smile. "Thanks, Sam," you say, and then add something about meeting us in two weeks to give us the complete report.

Sam's arms and energy pull us into our car. John's jaw is tight. He mutters, "Two weeks . . ."

Sam bounces in the backseat, kicks the upholstery, and wiggles the door lock switch. He is jabbering incessantly. I try to decipher his words but the sounds are all jumbled up with my thoughts: What did she learn about Sam? Will he catch up? Can we handle this? Is this forever?

Sam screeches his high-pitched squeal, the one that means "you're not listening to me." He's right. He's demanding our attention. Could he get a few extra points on his IQ test for being assertive with us? Isn't this an important sign of intelligence?

That evening, nothing goes right. Dinner burns to a smelly crisp, and every credit card company picks that moment to call. I feel so alone. I must visit the funeral home; my friend Linda's mother has died. As I stand in line to express my regrets, I feel Linda's sorrow and loss, but I feel my grief, too. My dreams for Sam are being challenged—some may die. Who will stand in line to console me? Who will even know?

I'm too tired to sleep. I sit up most of the night worrying. Dr. Gordon, what did you find? Two weeks? *Two weeks* until we know what you think about our Sam?

The Professional's Hidden Lyrics

I am glad we've reached the end of this session. Your child is tired and more than a little cranky. His eyes and tiny body are restless. He resists all my coaxing to get him to play with the blocks. It is time to stop.

He worked hard. I feel my fatigue, too. I offer him stickers, and he pushes through the pile, searching for the right one. Finally, he uncovers a train, of course. He seems delighted with his selection. I am glad. I lightly rub the back of my neck and am reminded how absorbed I become when I test a child. Sam tries to speed down the hall but I slow him down by reaching for his tiny wiggling hand. When we arrive in the waiting room, he rushes to show you his stickers.

I smile, but my heart is aching for you. Your child has just demonstrated significant delays in a number of areas—not just in language, not just in problem-solving, but also in motor development and some of the everyday living skills he should have acquired by now. Memory tasks were hard for him, and he could not manage some of the early conceptual reasoning items.

I am glad you brought Sam in for this assessment. I think my findings and your knowledge of your child will help identify some of the next steps and supports so he can reach his potential. But I am well aware that for you, these next steps will feel like climbing a steep mountain in the bitter cold.

I see you greet your child, Mr. and Mrs. Lewis. I know you want me to tell you something—or maybe everything—right now, right this very second. I can't. I need time to think about what I've learned and to prepare a report in a careful and useful manner.

I wonder how much you already realize. I worry that my findings will send arrows through your hearts.

A Few Ideas From the Parent Perspective

- Waiting for test results is the pits!
- Please prepare me for the challenge of waiting. Tell me some parents feel nervous, irritable, lonely, scared, or sad, that some withdraw for a while, that others feel a burst of energy and attempt to complete every task on their "to do" list. Suggest things I might do to help us through this waiting time.
- I know you need to consider carefully before you can give us results. For now, can you give us an inkling of hope or some feedback?
- It may be helpful if I'm reminded that I did the right thing by bringing my child in today.
- Give me information! Connect me to some helpful resources, other parents, agencies, reading materials. Don't underestimate the importance of these sources.

A Few Ideas From the Professional Perspective

- I know waiting is hard. I need time to review the test results and my observations of your child. I don't want to make quick judgments.
- If I am forced to delay this process, I will keep you informed and will do my best to complete the report in a timely fashion. I appreciate your understanding.
- I see many families, each with unique needs and desires. Some parents want lots of details; others want the main points and details later, over time. Some parents want to hear every score; others want information about their child with less attention to the scores. There is no one procedure that is right for all. If you know what is most comfortable for you, please let me know. I'll try to be sensitive to your wishes.
- I don't want children to be reduced to test scores. Know that I work to see the strengths and wonder of each child.

NOTES

SCENE 4

The Parent's Hidden Lyrics

How did your two weeks turn into three? I tried to be pleasant when the school called to say you had to reschedule—family illness, they said. But I didn't feel pleasant, just upset. This is our verdict. We need to know *now!*

Sam has stayed home with his grandma. As you lead John and me down the long hall to your office, you apologize for the delay and say it must have been hard to wait the extra week. That helps. I want to thank you for understanding, but I don't. It's too hard to juggle all my feelings.

I'm determined to listen, but my eyes fly away from your face to your floor, your walls, your diplomas, your bookcases where Sam gleefully found your books about trains and trucks. You lean toward us, and you start speaking without notes. I force myself to look at you and not the report on your desk. Your voice is direct. You look right into our eyes.

You describe Sam's "charming qualities" and you smile. I like your word, "charming." I remember the first time Sam saw Thomas the Train on TV. He was munching on his favorite food—homemade french fries with loads of ketchup. He charged right up to the screen to hear the talking train that rolled its big eyes. He was so excited he splattered ketchup all over his face and shirt. I chuckle aloud at the memory.

You fold your hands and consult your report. A torrent of words rushes at John and me, sweeping away my thoughts of Sam and his trains. Too many words—they all run together: Cognitiveimpairmentmotordelayreducedvisualmotorintegrativedyspraxia.

I think, "If I were a good mom I'd hear every word." I must be experiencing a motherhood malfunction. *Scored-in-the-fifth-percentile-on, scored-in-the-tenth-percentile-on, fourth percentile, seventh.* The words fly at jet speed right out of my head.

I feel tears brimming and I blink them back. I don't want to cry. Not here. *Not now!*

"You don't have to hear everything today," you say. "It's a lot to handle. We can talk again."

Your words stay with me. I'll replay them later. For the present, John and I reach for each other's hands. Silently we ask, "What do we do now?"

The Professional's Hidden Lyrics

I've been worrying about this meeting.

I chose this work because I wanted to make things better for children and their families, not worse. It is heart-wrenching to bring "life-changing news."

I've thought a lot about my report. How to be accurate and clear; gentle and helpful? How to capture on paper your engaging child with his strengths and his difficulties? How to write an insightful, professional report without breaking your hearts?

You both sit so bravely, so straight in your chairs. I begin by telling you that I was delighted to work with your child. "He has wonderful energy and a strong ability to connect with people. I chuckled each time he gleefully shouted, 'Sure!'" You smile with recognition when I describe Sam's loveable traits.

Then I move into the more formal findings. My words do not come easily. All the choices seem harsh: Challenged. Compromised. Diminished. Reduced for his age.

The paradox is that to help, I must hurt. In order to establish his eligibility for services, I must document his deficits. I worry. Will his strong points, his expressiveness and persistence, get buried under an avalanche of test scores and terminology?

You both nod, but your faces look stricken, hopeless. Tears appear in your eyes, Mrs. Lewis. You try to hold them back, but soon they're cascading down your face. I hesitate. Do I speak out loud to your tears? I want to reach out and touch you, but I don't know if that would be comfortable for you. What do you need right now? How can I help?

A Few Ideas From the Parent Perspective

- When you give us initial diagnosis or assessment results, choose a time when all the significant people are available. Let's talk about who I'd like to have present at this meeting.
- Please meet us when and where we can have privacy and no interruptions.
- Refer to my child by name. Tell me what you liked about him. When I sense your regard for him, I can hear your words better.
- Be honest with us. Don't hide what you know.
- Refrain from overwhelming us with volumes of details. Try not to project too far into the future, at least for now.
- Keep our hope afloat. Tell us about successes. We are gradually beginning to form new dreams and expectations.
- Give us as many resources as you can. It's best if you hand us written lists, brochures, and pamphlets to take with us. This may give us direction and hope.
- Be comfortable with our tears, our silence, our frustration, and our fears.
- Don't tell us, "It could be worse." As one parent said, "It could be better, too."
- Know that your sensitivity is a great comfort for us. You can't take away our strong feelings, but you can offer support and understanding. Never underestimate the power of listening and caring.

A Few Ideas From the Professional Perspective

- I want you to know that I would never intentionally be hurtful.
- Please know that it's normal for you to want all the answers, to know what the future will bring. After all, you are the child's parents. Unfortunately, I do not have all the answers, and the future is impossible to predict accurately. I will be honest with you, even

> Never underestimate the power of listening and caring.

though it may be hard to listen to the uncertainty. I encourage you to ask questions as frequently as you need to.

- If you feel unclear about a recommendation, or if you disagree with aspects of the report, let's talk about it. You know your child in hundreds of ways that no one else does: playing choo-choo train on the kitchen floor, dancing at Grandma Rose's party, swinging in your yard, eating his morning oatmeal, squealing in the backseat of the car. Your input is so very important. It helps me create a full and accurate picture of him.
- Know that in the real world of qualifying for services, the written report may need to emphasize his difficulties. I will remind you of this harsh reality and will do my best to include his strengths as well.
- If you feel I am rushing you through your feelings, please let me know. If I am going too slowly, let's talk it over. Our partnership works best when we guide each other.
- When you can, give me honest, constructive feedback about this process and my role in it.
- Understand that I want to help your child and support your efforts in every possible way.

SCENE 5

The Parent's Hidden Lyrics

It's been twenty-four hours since we sat in your school office, but it feels like a century. Nothing has changed, but everything feels different.

I glance up from my soggy cereal and cold cup of coffee. The calendar on the refrigerator reminds me: It's John's mother's birthday. My stomach knots. It will be the celebration of the decade. How can I possibly drag my body to Rose's party? How can I possibly face red balloons, colored streamers, smiling faces, kids chasing kids—*normal* kids chasing *normal* kids? How can John and I walk into that room pretending that we are just fine, thank you. That Sam is just fine, thank you. That our future will be just fine, thank you.

I can picture it now, the voices of my sisters-in-law: "Jennifer is so bright. We're sending her to the Montessori school." "Josh was reading when he was 3!" "Courtney's music teacher tells us she has unusual talent."

No one ever asks about Sam. They know something's not quite right, and it makes them awkward. Tonight we will stand in that room full of kind, well-meaning people, and no one will know what to say.

Dr. Gordon, it was hard to hear what you told us, but it was also a great relief to be able to talk with you. You don't know how lonely it's been, how worried I've been about Sam's delays, how alarmed I've been by his halting speech, how crushed I've been to see his sweet legs fail at running as fast as the other kids.

You had words and explanations for things I noticed in Sam a long time ago. Some of your words felt like new keys to locked doors. I piled the papers you gave us, the "additional resources for families," on my bedside stand. I can't read them yet . . . maybe not even next week.

But I will . . . when I'm ready.

The Professional's Hidden Lyrics

When I left my office yesterday evening, I was weighed down with loss and sadness. Those feelings lurk just around the corner today and appear unexpectedly while I am at the grocery store.

Two young mothers who obviously know each other are standing in the produce section. Their sons—about Sam's age—are chattering away. I move closer. One of the boys tells a silly joke, one of those jokes only funny to 5-year-olds, and the boys laugh raucously. Your child, I realize with sadness, would probably not understand such a joke.

The mothers' words float across the grapes and broccoli: "Mrs. Miller is a wonderful kindergarten teacher . . . most of her kids are reading by the end of the year and she really challenges kids in science and math, too! When Amanda had her, Mrs. Miller had them all building volcanoes!"

Could your child hold his own in such a class? Would such a setting welcome him? Could Mrs. Miller meet your child's needs, too? Sighing, I push my cart toward the deli section.

Mr. and Mrs. Lewis, you are at the beginning of a long journey. Yours is a trip with no road map and no end in sight. Will you be able to hold great expectations for your child as you learn more about his abilities and challenges? You see a child who has more capabilities than I saw— but, of course, you know him better than I do. Or, as the jargon goes, are you in denial? Is being in denial such a bad thing? Could it be necessary? Might it even be helpful? Maybe "denial" means you have the "pause button" pushed so you can slow down this process and absorb it bit by bit, frame by frame.

I wonder how you are feeling today. Are you prepared for heartbreaking reminders of your son's difficulties, even in the produce department? Will you still be able to see Sam's many gifts?

A Few Ideas From the Parent Perspective

- Please know there is more to my life than having a child with these delays, but right now I'm having a hard time thinking about anything else. I feel consumed by this. Life feels fragile.
- I might not be able to follow up immediately on your suggestions. It's not because I don't care or I'm "in denial." I need time and support to absorb all of this, to rearrange my dreams.
- Let me know if you learn about other resources, parent groups, or information that might be relevant to my search for understanding my child and what he needs.
- If you can phone me to see how I'm doing, it may help me feel less alone. I'm learning that many family members and friends may not know how to reach out to me during this challenging time. They worry that they may be intrusive. You, more than most people, have a sense of what I'm dealing with.

A Few Ideas From the Professional Perspective

- I really care about the children I meet. I want to be helpful to them and their families.
- If there is something I've done that was useful, please let me know. I can learn from your ideas and feedback.
- If something does not work, I want to know that, too. If any of the resources or referrals weren't useful or no longer existed, please inform me so I can better help you and others.
- My thoughts of your child and you, too, do not end when the test report is locked in my office. I like hearing how your child is doing.

NOTES

SCENE 6—SIX MONTHS LATER

The Parent's Hidden Lyrics

I linger outside the door to Sam's kindergarten classroom. It's my monthly afternoon to be a parent volunteer in his class. Before entering the room, I pause and sneak a glance at Sam through the tiny window in the closed door. I want to see how— or if—he interacts with the other kids. I want to know how he's doing in this "regular kindergarten with special supports for Sam." As I lean closer to the window glass, I'm surprised to see you, Dr. Gordon. You and Sam are digging in the sand table near the corner of the room. I can't make out your words, but I can tell you are trying to make Sam laugh. He does!

It's been months since you tested Sam. Queasiness in my stomach returns, reminding me of those earlier days in your office when John and I sat on those gray chairs near the bookshelf. We were hoping you would tell us, *in no uncertain terms,* that Sam would be just fine. That didn't happen.

My whole world turned upside down that day, but I am still standing. I have learned so much about Sam and the world of disabilities. I know about resources, and I am involved in getting the best services for Sam and our family. I've talked with two other moms who have children with developmental delays. These moms helped me to feel less alone and unsure of myself. They've introduced me to so many resources. I still have many worries about Sam. Some nights I wake up in a cold sweat. Sometimes, when I'm swinging Sam in the park, tears unexpectedly slide down my cheeks. But I also feel a renewed sense of myself. I feel a bit more confident, more determined. New dreams for Sam and our family are beginning to take shape.

Those first meetings with you were so hard. I didn't want to hear your words, yet I knew I had to listen. I remember that you called a week or two after giving us the results of his assessment. Your call and concern meant so much to us. You couldn't make Sam "catch up," but you did help ease some of the worry and sadness. You answered our questions thoroughly. You even helped us know what questions to ask. You led us to some helpful resources and parent groups.

The school bell rings, and I jump. It's time to go in. I open the door, greet Sam's teacher, and walk across the room. I decide to join you and Sam at the sand box. Sam screeches with delight when he sees me. We embrace and then shove our hands into the cold, wet sand. I touch Sam's pudgy fingers and wonder what we will build.

The Professional's Hidden Lyrics

Whenever I have a minute, I like to slip into the classroom and visit one of the children I've tested. Today, I am spending time with your child when you appear in his classroom. It is good to see you both.

Sam sparkles with his special exuberance for people. He is very sensitive to others. Today Shauna was longingly watching the other children at the sand table. They didn't pay attention to her, but your Sam called out cheerfully, "Shauna, Shauna, here!" and he handed her a shovel. It was just the invitation she needed.

Sam seems to be doing well in this class. Mrs. Katz has carefully adapted the kindergarten curriculum for your child so that he is both challenged and supported. I cannot help but wonder if next year's teacher will be as skilled in including him, and the next year's teacher, and the one after that? What lies ahead for him and you?

Mrs. Lewis, what is it like for you to visit this classroom where you see how much some of the children Sam's age can do? You look more "settled" today than the last time we met. But I would guess that pain and loss can be easily triggered for you, probably when you least expect it.

I want to stay longer, but I have a busy day ahead of me, with more meetings and evaluations. And this afternoon I see the Chandlers, another loving family with whom I must share difficult news.

A Few Ideas From the Parent Perspective

- I appreciate when you get in touch with me and ask about my child. Please continue to call me from time to time. Your interest means a lot to me.
- If you see my child at school, let me know how you think he is doing.

A Few Ideas From the Professional Perspective

- Encourage your child's teacher to invite me into the classroom. I can learn so much about your child's interests, needs, and relationships by visiting him there.
- Call me with any concerns you might have regarding your child's current program or his relationship with his peers.
- Tell me your thoughts about your child's school experience. Before we know it, we'll be planning for next year!

My Reflection: As you read the Story of Sam, what feelings did you experience? What do you hope to remember and use as you build partnerships?

THE STORY OF RACHEL

The Situation

Steve and Marci Goldstein are the parents of three children, 13-year-old Abby, 10-year-old Kevin, and 7-year-old Rachel. They're a close-knit and outdoorsy family—the kids share their parents' love of nature and have a collection of unusual pets, including Rachel's albino black snake, Snowflake. This has been a difficult time for the Goldstein family. Steve was laid off from his job at the factory two years ago. He tries to look at the bright side, saying it gives him more time with the kids, but still, it is stressful. Their worse fear is that they could lose their much-loved home. Steve and Marci want their three children to get a good education, but school never came easy to either of them, and neither went to college.

Abby, Kevin, and Rachel were all robust and healthy babies who developed typically. Each appeared ready for school and ready to learn. But while Abby and Kevin progressed easily through the early grades, Rachel's story is somewhat different.

Rachel was successful in kindergarten when presented with pre-academic tasks. In first grade, she enjoyed math and appeared to be a fluent reader. But while she was able to answer basic reading comprehension questions, abstract or challenging questions were met with hesitation or a simple shrug of the shoulders. Because of her good decoding skills, neither her teacher nor her parents noticed the problem.

Early in her second-grade year, Rachel's teacher, Mr. Crawford, noticed that although Rachel could add and subtract easily, she had trouble solving story problems in math. Although she was able to decode words with accuracy, it appeared that she was having difficulty in comprehending much of what she was reading. She seemed to be simply word calling.

Mr. Crawford met with the Goldsteins, who were surprised and concerned. They readily agreed to seek assistance from the school's Response to Intervention team (RtI). After hearing about Rachel's strengths, needs, and interests, this committee proposed strategies to support Rachel's reading at school and at home.

Although Mr. Crawford tried several of the interventions suggested, Rachel's reading comprehension did not improve. After six weeks, the RtI team next recommended that Rachel receive daily additional support in a small group setting, referred to as Academic Intervention Services (AIS). This was a general education service that would provide Rachel with individualized instruction to enhance her reading comprehension. The team planned to meet in four weeks to review the data gathered by the AIS teacher. Meanwhile, Mr. and Mrs. Goldstein worked painstakingly at home with their daughter. They were perplexed, as Rachel continued to read aloud flawlessly. While they were grateful for the attention and assistance she was receiving, they were confused and frustrated.

At the following RtI meeting, it was determined that despite the interventions, Rachel's reading comprehension was not improving. As a result, Rachel was referred for testing to determine if she was eligible for special education services.

Our Story's Design

These four scenes, which take place at pertinent points within the special education process, describe the feelings and interactions of the parents and the professionals as they worked together on behalf of Rachel.

As in the previous scenario, each scene is presented from two perspectives. We listen to the parent's internal thoughts and feelings—the hidden lyrics, as well as those of one of the professionals. Practical suggestions for both parents and professionals are included at the end of each scene, followed by a comprehensive list of suggestions in Chapter 4: The Dance Manual.

SCENE 1

The Parent's Hidden Lyrics

Since Abby started kindergarten nine years ago, Steve and I have been in this school building so many times. Nine years of open houses, conferences, concerts—I know this building like the back of my hand. I know the principal and most of the teachers, yet today I feel like I'm walking through these doors for the first time. Butterflies fill my stomach, and I reach for Steve's hand.

As we enter the main hallway, we are greeted warmly by you, Mrs. Sahouri. I never thought we'd be meeting with the school psychologist. You shake our hands and lead us into your office. It's a comfortable place, filled with children's artwork and stacks of games on the bookshelves. The upholstered chairs are welcoming but we sit rigidly, unable to relax. I notice the certificates and diplomas on the wall behind your desk, and I am reminded that I never made it to college. I wonder if you know that, or even care.

I can tell that you got to know Rachel when you comment on her amazing knowledge of snakes and other reptiles. You confide that you're terrified of snakes and we share a laugh, but my anxiety persists. I dread what's coming next, and yet I am curious. I want to know . . . and I don't want to know!

You seem to sense our discomfort, and you proceed slowly, yet it isn't long before I'm feeling overwhelmed. You name the tests that you will be using to "measure Rachel's cognitive ability." Next you tell us that Mrs. Hanson, the special education teacher, will administer standardized academic tests so that Rachel's cognitive ability can be compared to her actual achievement. All this testing! My head starts to spin.

Then you tell us that Miss DeWitt, the speech and language pathologist, "or SLP for short," you say, will also be conducting evaluations. "But why?" Steve asks. "Rachel speaks well. Everyone understands her!" You agree with him and explain that Miss DeWitt will be evaluating Rachel's ability to understand and process language, not the way she pronounces words. "OK, calm down." I say to myself, "Take a deep breath."

You must notice that I am uncomfortable. You shift in your chair, move forward a bit and say, "We're just trying to understand why Rachel is having difficulty. Hopefully, these evaluations will give us a clue." Steve nods. I muster a stiff smile.

You tell us that when the testing is completed, we'll all meet to discuss the results of the evaluations and the next steps. You call the meeting something with letters in it . . . like *e*'s and *p*'s. I have such a hard time remembering this special ed lingo.

Next, you bring out a social history form and ask lots of questions about Rachel's history, when she first walked and talked, her illnesses, injuries, operations, allergies, and so on. We answer as best as we can, certain that we must be leaving out something. Here's what I feel like saying: Rachel is smart and always has been. She knew the alphabet by the time she was 2. She could count to one-hundred when she was just 4. Her handwriting is nicer than Steve's, and she reads better than Abby and Kevin did at her age. How could she have a disability? This whole thing feels unreal! And then, out of the blue, I silently am hit with the thought, "How is this going to affect Rachel's future . . . her work, her friendships, her life . . ." My head is racing into Rachel's future . . . I catch myself and force myself to be *here*, now, in your office.

I ask about the next meeting date. You explain that by law, it must be held within 60 days. *"Sixty days!* Why so long?" I don't say that out loud. I just think it. Sure you have lots to do, but this is our child . . . and that's two months away.

You give us a handbook, "Parents' Guide to Special Education" and tell us to read it at home. You say it explains our right to due process if we disagree with the decisions made by the IEP team. I think, "What is due process?" You add, "As parents, you will be a part of the IEP team, a very important part of the team." I wonder how I can be on this team if I can't even talk like you, if I don't understand your rules or words.

You say that you'll call us and we'll meet after the testing is completed.

"Before sixty days?" I ask. "Definitely," you say, wanting to reassure me.

Steve and I get up, shake your hand, and thank you. Right now, I just want to be sitting on my front porch, watching the kids shoot hoops in our driveway.

Steve and I don't say much on the way home. I wonder if he thinks Rachel's problems are my fault. My oldest brother was in special education years ago. My mind continues wandering. Maybe Steve has something to do with this. His layoff has been hard on all of us. Maybe that's why Rachel can't recall what she reads.

This is not an easy place to be.

The Professional's Hidden Lyrics

I look out the window in the main office and see you, Mr. and Mrs. Goldstein, walking to the entrance holding hands. As a newlywed, I smile and hope that my husband and I will still be holding hands twenty years from now.

You greet me politely and try to smile, but I can sense your apprehension. I recognize your faces; you are "regulars" here at school, but I realize that there is nothing regular about today. Rachel's situation is a new one for you. You must feel like you are treading in unknown waters.

In my office, you gaze at the children's artwork and sit stiffly at my desk. I try to make you feel comfortable by talking about Rachel and her interest in reptiles. When you smile, Mr. Goldstein, I see Rachel's toothless grin. I must remember to tell you that next time.

I explain the referral process and the timeline, and talk about all the testing that will be conducted. I say "special education services" and you, Mrs. Goldstein, blanch. I wish I didn't have to say those words because I see how much it upsets you. I have to remember that we teachers are so familiar with this process and all the jargon. I remind myself to use less jargon, and as my husband would say, "talk like regular folks."

I wish we had learned more about talking with parents when I was in college. So much emphasis was placed on testing and report writing. I know I'm good at that part, but connecting with parents is important, too. I don't want you to see me as the enemy. I want you to trust me and know that I care.

I lean closer to you and say that we're trying to understand why Rachel is having difficulty, and that maybe these evaluations will give us a clue. I wonder if you hear me. Maybe I should have said, "We are trying to discover more about Rachel's unique way of learning." Is that easier to hear?

Next comes the paperwork, which includes the "consent to evaluate" and the social history, a long and probing document that even asks how long you were in labor. Interestingly enough, you seem to enjoy answering those questions. You chuckle together over the chicken pox that ran through each of your children one by one . . . for more weeks than you care to remember. You reminisce about Rachel's first words, first steps, and first attempts at using the potty.

You seem to want to tell me about Rachel. Your willingness to share is helpful. I can't do my work without your input and ideas. "Don't hold back," I want to say. "Trust me. I need to hear what you know." I remind myself not to talk so much, to go slower. I want to hear what you say.

I know this is hard for you. Part of me wants to empathize and speak soothing words, but another part says "keep your professional distance." So I just smile and review all the paperwork. I end with telling you about the next steps and the next meeting. I hope you know that I will do my best.

A Few Ideas From the Parent Perspective

- Remember that I am new to this. I want to understand everything you are saying, but all this new information and unfamiliar jargon can be overwhelming. If I become quiet or don't ask questions, it's not that I don't care. I just need some time.
- It really helps when you slow down and give me time to think about my questions. Remind me that I don't have to understand everything at this time.
- I want to tell you what I know about my child. Encourage me to share my stories about her in my own way.
- I need time to know if I can trust you.
- Allow me time to think about this new information. If I feel pushed, even if you don't mean to, or if I feel you are trying to convince me to see it your way, I may stop listening or become uncomfortable.
- Know that I appreciate your kindness and, most importantly, your listening.

A Few Ideas From the Professional Perspective

- I want to learn all I can about your child.
- We want to have a complete picture and understanding about your child, which is why we ask you to bring in whatever information you have about your child's past milestones (when your child walked, talked, etc.), illnesses, interests, and so on.
- Professionals often use specialized language. Stop me if I use jargon, words, or acronyms that are unfamiliar to you. I will gladly explain them.
- I am required to give you some written information, such as the *Parents' Handbook and Procedural Safeguards,* but I don't want to overwhelm you with too much reading. Some parents like receiving lots of written information and resources; others want less or want it in other formats such as e-mail. Let me know what works best for you.
- It's never easy to wait for test results. I wish I could provide them immediately, but I am balancing many assignments. I will give you a timeline so you know what to expect, and when. But as always, if you need to talk to me between scheduled meetings, just contact me.
- Ask, ask, and ask again. It is your right to understand each step of the process. Your questions help me know what you need to be fully involved in this process.

SCENE 2

The Parent's Hidden Lyrics

Once again, we march up the concrete steps to the main entrance of the school, and once again, I'm nervous. It's been three weeks since the testing began, and every day I've waited for *the* call. I know that there have been three separate evaluations conducted by three different professionals who have many responsibilities, but that hasn't made the wait any easier.

You, Mrs. Sahouri, meet us as we sign in, and we chat about the school's new outdoor basketball courts as we head toward your office. When we get there, I'm surprised to find it empty, as I was expecting Mrs. Hanson and Miss DeWitt. You explain that they will be meeting with us separately. I'm grateful for this act of thoughtfulness; listening to three reports at one time would surely be overwhelming.

We sit down at your table and see the test manual and three copies of your report waiting for us. You patiently review the test with us, explaining what each part measures. You give us examples by reading various questions and telling us how Rachel answered. I inwardly chuckle when you tell us how Rachel answered the question about "the perfect pet."

You tell us what she did well . . . Suddenly I hear unfamiliar words coming at me, as if you are speaking a foreign language. You use words and numbers faster than I can take in. *Standard scores . . . 90–110 . . . average range . . . 80–90 low . . . average range . . . 110–120 . . . high average range.* Again, my head is spinning.

Steve asks, "Who decides what is average, low, and high?" It gives me a chance to take a deep breath. You put Rachel's scores on a chart that has a curve, and show us that most of her scores are in the average or high average ranges. The only scores in the low average range are "comprehension" and "working memory." I struggle to understand. I am determined to make sense of all your words and numbers. And then, out of nowhere, I feel this surge of love for Rachel. I want to hug her. I want to shield her—and myself too—from these lines and curves and questions. What does all this mean for Rachel?

I can tell you want to do a good job of explaining this to us. You say that Rachel's cognitive ability is in the average range. I want to say, "Of course, we knew that!" You continue, "But she hasn't been responding to the intervention—the weeks of tutoring from the AIS teacher. That's why we need to look at her language and academic scores. If she is a child with average ability, then her expected achievement is average. Your words start to blend into one large word, *expected-actual-discrepancy-tests*.

Steve and I look at each other. We're confused. I want to ask really smart questions but don't know what they are. What I do know is that the words *learning disability* is echoing through the room. Perhaps being numb at this moment is a good thing.

You ask if we have any questions. About a million, I think, but shake my head. You tell us to call with any questions we might have after meeting with Mrs. Hanson and Miss DeWitt. We grip each other's hands and cross the hall to Mrs. Hanson's room, where more news awaits us.

NOTES

The Professional's Hidden Lyrics

"What a roller-coaster ride this is going to be for you," I think to myself, as I watch you approach. My news will be good, but Mrs. Hanson's and Miss DeWitt's . . .

We meet as you sign in and head for my office. You're surprised that we're meeting alone, but your shoulders seem to soften. You settle in nervously, and I describe the tests that I administered to your daughter. You listen to the questions and try to predict how Rachel would have answered. As I share some of her responses, you smile and seem to relax a bit. "That's so Rachel!" you say several times.

I show you Rachel's scores and try to explain what these numbers actually mean. You, Mr. Goldstein, ask a few questions and I answer as best I can, but I sense your confusion. This is the hard part of my job. I understand how these numbers and charts can help us understand Rachel. But I still struggle with how best to help families understand all of this clinical material. I keep trying new ways . . . I go on to explain about the other evaluations: the expected achievement scores, the meaning of significant discrepancies. You, Mrs. Goldstein, sit so quietly, but I see you stiffen when you hear the words "learning disability." Is that all you are hearing? I want you to understand all of my explanations.

I've learned to take my cues from parents, so I stop and remind myself not to bombard you with too much information at this first meeting. I try to read your facial expressions . . . are you relieved, doubtful, scared, angry, sad? Do you trust me? I know that you'll be receiving more detailed information about Rachel's challenges from Mrs. Hanson and Miss DeWitt. I wonder how you will handle that news. All I can do is offer my help, if you need it or want it.

A Few Ideas From the Parent Perspective

- There's no way around it—this kind of meeting is hard.
- I want to understand what you are learning about my child, but I don't want my child to get lost in your charts, jargon, and tests. I want to take home the child I love, not a label.
- Begin our conversation with a story or two of what my child does well, or what you enjoyed about my child. I need to know if you know the child I know.
- Remind me that your tests are only one way of understanding my child.
- Eventually, I might want to know all the details of your testing, but probably not at this first meeting. Right now I mainly want to learn what my child does well and how we can support her to grow and learn as best she can.
- Don't get frustrated with me if I question you, disagree with you, or want other opinions.
- Find out what is important to our family.
- Give me some time to adjust to this information

A Few Ideas From the Professional Perspective

- I appreciate your patience as you wait for all of your child's evaluations and reports to be completed. I know that waiting isn't easy. Some days I wish you were the only family I am working with, but as you can guess, that's not the situation. I have several responsibilities, including providing counseling to many students in different schools. I also do many evaluations, complete the written reports, and meet with families and students. As a psychologist, I also consult with teachers, therapists, administrators, and parents and attend many meetings. Each member of the team has similar responsibilities.
- It might be helpful to bring a notepad for taking notes when we discuss the results of your child's evaluations. I also want you to feel comfortable jotting down notes on the written report itself. The other evaluators and I can easily print you a clean copy.

- Ask as many questions as you want. Like all new experiences, it takes time to fully understand what is being said. Know that you'll become more confident as you experience and learn more.
- Remember that the evaluations we use are just one tool to understand your child's learning. There are many other ways to learn about your child's abilities. That's why your input is valuable.
- At home, consider rereading the reports. Take your time. You don't have to review them immediately.
- Think through the suggestions made by the professionals. Some ideas might immediately make sense for your family and your routines. Others might not be a perfect match. I look forward to talking about these with you over time.

SCENE 3

The Parent's Hidden Lyrics

Two more weeks have passed, and today is Rachel's eligibility meeting. . . . I can't believe that I am now using their language . . . IEP! Steve and I have reread all three of Rachel's reports and the *Parents' Guide to Special Education*—well, at least a few of its pages. The laws and technical language are hard to understand, but we want to be the best parents we can be, so we keep trying.

We're glad you connected us with the parent group. It was helpful to talk with another mother whose child is receiving special education services. She knew . . . she just knew what we were going through and had some good tips. We didn't talk long, but it was a beginning. But even with all of that preparation, we're anxious.

How am I supposed to look as a mother attending her child's first IEP meeting? I feel like I am back in middle school as I search my closet for the right thing to wear . . . do all mothers go through this? I finally choose my most comfortable sweater as I hear Steve honk the horn in the driveway. I am glad that this old car of ours started up without stalling.

We rush to the school building, sign in, and sit down in the main office. In what seems like just a moment, we are warmly greeted by you, Mrs. Liu, the director of special education. You invite us to follow you into the conference room, where the team members are gathering.

The sun is streaming into the large room, making it feel cheery and taking some of the edge off my jangled nerves. You ask us to sit next to you and across from Rachel's teachers. I wish I could remember everyone's name. There are so many of you, and only two of us. We settle into the large comfortable chairs around the conference table. Steve taps my shoe with his.

You, Mrs. Liu, open the meeting by having everyone introduce themselves. Then you pull out some photos of Rachel, place them on the table, and remind the group that she's the reason we are here. I feel a rush of appreciation. What a great idea, Mrs. Liu!

You begin by asking Steve and me to tell the team all about Rachel. There's that word again, "team." Is this really a team? It certainly isn't the kind of team Steve wants to be a part of . . . a hockey team would be his preference. But we want to give it our best, so we settle into the meeting.

Where do I start? There is so much to say about Rachel. Steve begins, but it's obvious that he's not sure exactly what you are looking for.

As if you read our minds, you offer a few questions, "What does Rachel seem to really enjoy doing? When does she shine? What do you want us to be sure we know about her?" Steve speaks easily about her fascination with snakes and her kindness to others. Mr. Crawford chimes in with some classroom stories. My heart swells with pride as he talks about the day Rachel brought her snake, Snowflake, for show and tell, and the time she skipped recess to comfort a classmate who was crying.

I wish we could talk about Rachel's wonderful qualities all day, but soon we're on to other matters. My anxiety comes flooding back as Mrs. Hanson and Miss DeWitt review the results of the tests. Miss DeWitt uses a term I don't understand, but I'm too rattled to ask for an explanation. I try to calm myself with the new mantra a friend taught me: Be patient. It will come with time.

Although I know these test results, I am strangely hoping that the bottom line will be different . . . but it isn't. You, Mrs. Liu, summarize what has been reported. You go on to say something about expected and actual achievement, but all I hear is ". . . in spite of the interventions, Rachel has failed to improve."

Rachel failed.

I want to call out, "maybe Rachel hasn't failed . . . maybe *you* have failed . . . or maybe we all have failed." I don't say those things. I only think them and feel the tears start to gather. You glance at me and seem to realize how harsh your words sounded. You clear your throat and start over, "Rachel has tried hard but the interventions so far haven't helped her. The tests indicate that there's a gap . . ." I blink back the tears. Then I hear more words: *the law . . . the disability.* I think, "What does the law have to do with Rachel? She's not broken any laws!"

I remind myself, "deep breath in and deep breath out."

Then the word, *disability* instantly fills the entire room, like smoke fills a burning house.

I look at you and hear you say, "It seems that the time has come to 'classify' Rachel." I shudder at that clinical-sounding term. The atmosphere somehow becomes more formal as you ask if everyone agrees that our daughter should be classified as a student with a learning disability.

Suddenly the face of my brother in his fifth-grade special ed class pops into my mind. I'm right back in our old elementary school, walking down the hall, trying to peek into his classroom. I see him in the corner all by himself.

More images swirl through my mind . . . my brother, my mother's worries, and now my worries for Rachel. What does her future hold? I shake my head and force myself to return to *now*, back to this room, back to "classifying" Rachel.

I hear everyone answering your question with a *yes.* I can only nod. I guess that makes it official . . . Rachel is now classified as a student with a learning disability. I knew this was coming, but it's so difficult to hear the words. I try to remain poised, try to blink away the tears. You hand me a tissue. You've done this before.

With this part of the meeting completed, you seem to heave a sigh of relief. In a brisk and upbeat tone, you ask the committee, "Now, how are we going to help Rachel?" You describe our options and list them on a flip chart.

Suddenly we're moving too fast, and while I struggle to keep up, I realize that something's not right. I raise my hand and say, "It looks like you're planning to pull her out of her classroom. That's not what we expected." You explain that the district inclusion program begins in third grade, and that first and second graders are usually pulled out. My heart begins to pound. "I don't agree with that! She's already being pulled out for the AIS. We don't want her being pulled out for more reading help." Steve looks at me with questioning eyes. I feel the heat in my cheeks—they must be beet red. "We really believe that Rachel should stay with her class. Our older two were in classes with kids with . . . disabilities . . . and they did great. They learned that everyone has different ways of learning."

You repeat that the district believes in the benefits of inclusive classrooms. However, you say, "Our younger children tend to need more intense individualized special education instruction, and that's why we provide a specialized program at that level. It's an excellent model."

I pause, and Steve jumps in. "No, we didn't expect this different classroom idea. Really, we are against it. We know Rachel. It would be terrible for her to be moved out of her classroom. Those kids are her friends."

The school psychologist, or is it the social worker . . . I can't keep all of these names straight . . . she says that she is confident that Rachel will make this transition. I feel my stomach clench. She doesn't need any more transitions. Transitions are stressful. I know that Rachel can succeed in the regular classroom with just a little more help.

And so we collide and campaign, back and forth. We know what is best for our daughter. And you all seem to think you know what is best for our daughter. Tension is rising around the table, and I'm grateful when Mrs. Liu calls for a ten-minute break to catch our breath.

We return to the conference room in awkward silence, and I wonder how we'll ever reach a resolution. Finally Mrs. Hanson, the special ed teacher, clears her throat and proposes a new idea. Maybe she could serve as a "teacher consultant" for Rachel.

When we ask what she means, she explains that she would be willing to coach the AIS teacher in strategies and techniques, and also meet with Rachel once a week during AIS to see how those strategies are working.

You, Mrs. Liu, seem to like the idea. And it certainly sounds right to us. I think it means that Rachel could stay where she belongs.

I ask again, just to be sure. "You mean Rachel can get special ed help while she is in her reading group and can stay in her regular class?"

You smile and answer "yes."

I am relieved that this issue was resolved today. You again ask if everyone is in agreement, and consensus is reached.

I know it sounds odd, but I feel a sudden peace come over me. Maybe it's the roller coaster stopping for a few moments. Steve and I may not know all of these words and tests, but we do know what's best for our daughter.

The rest of the meeting goes a bit more smoothly, though I still would rather be someplace else. We develop Rachel's IEP and discuss supports and testing accommodations and agree on a starting date. We say we'd like to take the papers home, read through them one more time and then sign them. You, Mrs. Liu, say that's fine, though I see the teacher whose name I can't recall fidget in her seat.

As we get up to leave, you shake Steve's hand, and then take my hands in yours and tell me that you look forward to working with us. I say honestly, "Me too."

The Professional's Hidden Lyrics

It's another eligibility meeting at Kennedy Elementary. I hope it goes well! I've been the director of special education for the past twenty years and have conducted thousands of such meetings. Parents can be nervous about these meetings. I empathize with them and try to make their difficult situation a little easier. I really believe in collaboration and partnership. I have so many partners, and each "dance" is unique. I look forward to meeting my newest partners.

I see Steve and Marci Goldstein waiting solemnly in the office. I greet them with a smile and invite them to join me and the others around the conference table.

I enjoy beginning these meetings by asking parents to tell us about their child. I feel that this puts them at ease and provides us all with important information. When Steve hesitates, I realize that perhaps I should give him a bit more direction. These big, broad questions can be overwhelming to parents who already feel outnumbered at such meetings.

The classroom teacher begins his report with positive comments about Rachel and then goes on to state the problem and how inter-vention has not helped. The evaluators review their findings. Then comes the hard part. Eligibility, I know, will not be controversial, but the act of classification is something else. Labels have meaning, but too often they are used in the wrong ways, or are used to think of a child in only one way. Parents' reactions can vary from a sense of shock or sadness to ultimate relief since now there is direction as to what can be done to support the child. Some initially think that special education will cure their child . . . I always want to say to parents, "Your child doesn't need curing or fixing. She needs sup-port, and that's what we are going to discover together."

Mrs. Goldstein, you bite your lip and try to remain calm, but your eyes tear up despite your efforts. When we formally identify Rachel as a student with a learning disability, I see your discom-fort. I hand you a tissue as I've done for other parents.

Finally comes the part that I love, finding the ways to help the child. You're disappointed that we don't have inclusive classes at the second-grade level and you make it clear that you do not want a pullout program.

The air thickens as the campaigning begins. I hold my tongue and allow each side to share their opinions. It has taken me years to believe in the necessity of conversation. We can't expect immediate agreement all the time, though I often long for it!

When this conversation goes on longer than most and becomes heated, I begin to worry that perhaps we won't reach an agreement today. I call for a break, hoping that a solution will appear when everyone is calmer.

When we return to the table ten minutes later, Mrs. Hanson cleverly suggests the idea of teacher consultant services provided during AIS. I am impressed by her creative solution and hope you like it, too. Your face brightens as you understand that Rachel will receive the necessary instruction and continue to remain in her second grade classroom. You and your husband agree with this plan and I feel a surge of relief. We're almost there.

Miss DeWitt recommends speech/language therapy to enhance Rachel's auditory processing skills and strengthen her receptive language ability, which hopefully, will improve her reading comprehension. It clicks! You realize that this is what Rachel needs, and you seem to be on board!

When we move on to develop Rachel's IEP, you listen attentively and contribute meaningfully. As our meeting draws to a close, I sense that you are at peace with both the process and the outcome. We worked through some difficulties and found solutions. Our partnership has begun.

A Few Ideas From the Parent Perspective

- Prepare me for the IEP eligibility meeting by telling me ahead of time what to expect. Who will be there? What procedures will we follow?
- This first IEP meeting is new and unfamiliar. It helps if you are friendly and welcoming. Maybe have a pitcher of water or a pot of coffee.
- Much of the numbers and data are confusing to me. Please go slowly and explain each score's significance along the way. The numbers don't mean a lot to me right now. Your concrete examples are much more helpful to us.
- I know my child better than anyone else does. Have respect for my opinions and suggestions; they are all based on love for my child.
- I may hesitate to ask questions, especially if I feel confused at times. Keep encouraging me to ask questions.
- Help me understand the correct terms and jargon, but don't expect me to speak your language, especially at first. Encourage me to express myself in my own words.
- Don't lower your expectations for my child because of her new label.
- Please give me time to review papers and documents at home if I request it.

A Few Ideas From the Professional Perspective

- You may not believe this, but I'm a little nervous too! No two IEP meetings are alike, and I want this to be a positive experience for all of us.
- Please come prepared to tell the team about your child. Bring photos if you like.
- Don't keep it all in your head. Take notes at the meeting, bring notes from home. A list of written goals can be very helpful.
- Many parents find it helpful to keep one folder or binder to hold all the notes, reports, and other information about their child.

- Several professionals will be reviewing the results of your child's evaluations. As we move forward in our partnership, let us know if detailed scores are important to you or if you would prefer a summary.
- Don't hesitate to ask questions. I welcome them at any time.
- Classification is a part of the formal process. It doesn't mean that I see your child as a "label." This is just one step toward getting the right support.
- I want to know what you want for your child. Tell me, and make sure I understand.
- We may not always agree on the best approach for your child. That's normal. Be patient with the discussion process. Sometimes finding the right solution takes time.
- Hold on to your dreams for your child. Great expectations foster success.

NOTES

SCENE 4

The Parent's Hidden Lyrics

I can't believe that it's June and the school year is about to end. Abby is finishing middle school, Kevin is finishing elementary school, and Rachel is finishing second grade with two new front teeth! She has been receiving teacher consultant services and speech/language therapy since January. I still worry but I guess that comes with being a mother. She does seem to laugh more at home.

Steve and I are on our way to Rachel's annual review meeting, and I'm anxious to hear the teachers' accounts of her progress. I'm almost excited to be going to this meeting! I've been communicating frequently with Mr. Crawford, Mrs. Hanson, Miss DeWitt and Mrs. Liu. We are all novices in our partnership, and though there have been some uncomfortable moments, we're improving as we go along. We arrive at school, sign in, and head to the conference room.

We enter the room filled with many familiar faces. You, Mrs. Liu, warmly greet us and invite us to sit in those comfortable chairs. As is your style and practice, you welcome everyone to Rachel's annual review meeting, and ask everyone present to introduce himself or herself. I am feeling hopeful about today's meeting.

You ask us how we think Rachel's year has gone, and Steve replies that since she's been receiving services, she seems happier. You, Mr. Crawford, tell the IEP team that Rachel appears to be more confident and no longer avoids eye contact when questions are posed. You tell us that you call on her first when you know that she is able to answer a specific question, so that no one else can "take her answer." By so doing, you, Mr. Crawford, have enhanced her self-confidence, and I can't thank you enough! You seem to blush at my praise and graciously give the credit to Mrs. Hanson, the special education teacher, who has provided you with suggestions and strategies to foster Rachel's success.

You, Miss DeWitt, have been providing speech/language therapy, as you say, to "improve Rachel's auditory processing and receptive language skills." I still wonder if I really understand what you mean by those words. . . . You acknowledge the work Steve and I are doing with Rachel at home. I appreciate your feedback!

You, Mrs. Hanson, produce your data and state that updated standardized testing indicates a slight improvement in reading comprehension. I try to ignore the word "slight" and focus on the word "improvement." It doesn't sound like much, but it's something. I look at Steve and smile.

This meeting is much easier, partly because Mrs. Liu called us ahead of time for what she called a pre-IEP phone call. (I joked with her that special education had a new name for everything!) She asked us for our input about how this year was for Rachel. What went well? What needs improvement? What do we want for her next school year?" It was helpful to talk about these things *before* the meeting. We sit, once again at the big table, but this time feeling more prepared, involved, and, I dare say, confident.

We discuss Rachel's current levels of performance. The "Rachel stories" that the staff members tell about her are music to my ears! Next, we discuss and establish the goals that we hope she'll achieve. We look at her current program and testing accommodations, and determine their appropriateness. Finally, we discuss accommodations and services for third grade.

I steel myself, and once again request a co-taught general education class, one with two teachers: a special education and general education teacher. You, Mrs. Liu, smile and agree. I heave a sigh of relief and glance around the table. No objections! I squeeze Steve's hand and grin. You, Miss DeWitt, want to maintain speech/language services and Steve voices our appreciation.

You, Mrs. Liu, review our plan for next year and ask if everyone is in agreement. My partners and I say *yes.*

NOTES

The Professional's Hidden Lyrics

It's a beautiful June day, and I only have 47 more annual reviews to conduct! As the IEP team gathers in the conference room, they greet each other warmly. Several months have passed since Rachel began receiving special education services, and what I sometimes call the "dance of partnership" has commenced.

The teachers have been forthright in their communication, discussing Rachel's progress and ongoing challenges. Over the past few months, parents and staff have discussed issues before they became problems. We continue to iron out our differences, working toward trust and respect for each other's points of view. It's amazing how much work this takes . . . for all of us.

As we meet today to discuss Rachel's progress and to develop her IEP for the upcoming year, I hope that our relationship will continue to thrive and move forward. I guess, to be realistic, we'll step on each other toes—and feelings—at times, but what relationship doesn't take work?

As we develop Rachel's IEP, I listen to your ideas as well as to those of the other team members. Together we create goals for Rachel in the areas of auditory processing, receptive language, and reading comprehension. I pause for a quick moment and realize, for the millionth time, how easily all these terms roll off my tongue. My husband jokes with me, "You know you really are bilingual . . . English and 'special education.'"

You pause, Marci, and seem to gather your courage. Then you tell me that you and Steve feel strongly that Rachel should continue in an inclusive co-taught class. I smile and concur wholeheartedly. The team nods in agreement, and heaving a sigh of relief, you reach for your husband's hand. You realize that we are on the same page, partners who will continue to work side by side with Rachel's best interests at heart.

We are progressing onto the next level of partnership. Together, we'll explore new ideas and options, and together, we'll watch Rachel grow and thrive.

A Few Ideas From the Parent Perspective

- Help me prepare for this very important meeting. A phone conversation with you several days before the meeting will help me organize our own thoughts and plans. Let me know what to expect and specific ways that I can be prepared to plan for next year.
- A helpful way to begin the meetings is hearing a few short stories about our child's progress and what has worked well this year. We can talk about other issues during the meeting.
- As you share how our child is doing, show us examples of her work.
- During the meeting, ask us about our goals for the coming year. Encourage us to participate by asking for and listening to our ideas. Show us that our thoughts are welcomed, even when they might not be exactly the same as yours.
- Let us know that you recognize that our child's progress is based on what happens in school, in our home, and in our community. It is helpful to hear about specific things that we did to support our child's growth and progress.
- Remind us that not all skills and progress "show up" immediately. Help us understand the important steps our child is making toward the bigger goals.

A Few Ideas From the Professional Perspective

- Come to this meeting prepared to share your feelings and observations about this year. Please be honest and forthright. I want to know what worked and what didn't, what were the challenges, and what was helpful to your child and to you.
- If there is something in particular that the staff did this year that was helpful, let us know so we can continue these efforts.
- Continue to be an active participant throughout each year by sharing information, ideas, stories, suggestions, and questions.
- Let's make a list of a few of our best ideas and "lessons learned" from this year and share it with next year's team. This can serve as bridge between the two years.

My Reflection: As you read the Story of Rachel, what feelings did you experience? What do you hope to remember and use as you build partnerships?

MORE RESOURCES

Los Angeles School District – Video: I.E.P. and You
http://sped.lausd.net/sepg2s/parents/iepprocess/en_video/
iepprocess_en.html

IDEA 2004: Federal legislation in Special Education
http://idea.ed.gov/explore/view/p/%2Croot%2Cdynamic%
2Cvideoclips%2C

The National Center on Response to Intervention
http://www.rti4success.org

CHAPTER THREE

The Dance Manual

Essential Steps to Keep on Dancing

In this chapter we present the essential steps necessary to create and maintain strong partnerships. These steps, identified separately for professionals and parents, are the basics, the building blocks, the fundamentals, for working together.

Visit this list of suggestions often and share it with parents and professionals during any phase of the partnership: at the beginning, during transitions, if challenges arise . . . any time we collide or begin to slide. We won't use every step at every dance with every partner, but a working knowledge of these basics can keep us gliding along.

FOR PARENTS: ESSENTIAL STEPS

In addition to these essential dance steps for parents to consider, we also share our thoughts about the absolute importance for parents to hold onto great expectations and hope.

> Share your dreams, high expectations, and hopes for your child and engage others to share.

Essential Dance Steps

- Go slow. It takes time to absorb new information, especially during the initial phases or at transitions or changes with partners. Don't expect to understand every detail, every report, or every choice immediately. Give yourself time to feel, think, question, and take in the new information. Don't do it alone. Seek out other parents, resources, organizations, family members and friends. (See page 138 for a list of resources.) Let a trusted person know what you are going through and how they might support you (i.e., by listening, going out to a baseball game, coming to a meeting with you, babysitting, bringing over a meal, or helping research a topic). Asking for support is a healthy thing to do, and a way to become a stronger partner.
- Ask for input from professionals. If you aren't sure what you need to know, try asking, "What are typical questions parents have asked about this assessment, these results, or these strategies?"
- Trust yourself. Don't dismiss or underestimate what you know about your child.
- Trust that your partners want to share valuable information with you and do their best to support your child.
- Communicate. Share what you know—you don't have to use the same words as professionals. Find *your* own words to tell stories about your child, about his or her abilities, and what's important to your family. You can use photos or other ways to share information. Words are only one way.
- Be prepared. To be ready for meetings, formal or informal, ask ahead of time what to expect, what to bring, and what

you should be prepared to talk about. Ask for a brief overview of the meeting, including the length and who will be present. Bring a list of thoughts, questions, and expectations you wish to address.

- Read carefully. Take your time reviewing the written reports. Remember that these reports can be useful as well as intimidating or overwhelming. Some parents find that reading them with a family member, a seasoned parent or peer mentor, a friend, or trusted professional is helpful.
- Ask. Your questions are important. If you're not sure how to phrase a question, try this: "I'm not sure I understand what you said. Could you repeat it, or give me another example?"
- Speak out. Express your opinions, thoughts, agreements, and disagreements with respect. If you are hesitant, for whatever reason, to share your thoughts at a meeting, follow up after the meeting with a one-on-one conversation or phone call with one of the professionals. You bring the much-needed family perspective.
- Take five. If you feel anxious or frustrated during conversations, it's OK to ask for a short break.
- Aim high. Keep your expectations high for your children. Resist the pull to limit their dreams. Our children are so much more capable than we might think. Share your dreams, high expectations, and hopes for your child and engage others to share.[1]
- Learn. With the help of professionals, families, and peers, discover how your child learns best. Familiarize yourself with the concept of multiple intelligences (Gardner, 2006) so that you can understand your child's learning style. Gardner, a pioneer in understanding the different types of intelligences teaches us that we are all smart in different ways.

---

[1] An effective planning tool is MAPS (Making Action Plans) developed by Jack Pearpoint, Marsha Forest, and others affiliated with The Marsha Forest Centre (www.inclusion.com). This tool asks eight key questions that assist in planning for the child's future. Questions include: *What are your dreams? What are your nightmares? What are the gifts and talents of this child? What steps are needed to build the dream and avoid the nightmare?*

- Share your family's cultural values, traditions, and routines. You have a lot to teach and share with professionals, not only about your child but also about your family and community.
- Give feedback. Let professionals know specifically what they did that was helpful, valuable, and appreciated.
- Involve your child. As your child grows, learn more about ways to include him or her in the meetings, planning, and discussions. A primary role of parents is to support their children to understand their disability, to know what supports and interventions they need, and how to advocate for themselves.
- Remember that your child is the same unique, wonderful child she or he was before the assessments.
- Be kind to yourself. Parenting is joyful and challenging. To sustain your energy for the long run, it's important to find ways to relax and step away from your parent role for a while.

My Reflection: As I review this list, the three that caught my attention are

An additional suggestion I want to add to this list is

A Word About Dreams, High Expectations, and Hope: The Most Essential Dance Steps

(from Janice)

When we first learned that our son Micah had a disability, we were stunned, worried and frightened . . . to name just a few of our emotions. It took time for us to adjust to this life-changing news. At first we thought that we had to give up—or drastically alter—our dreams for Micah. However, with the support and wisdom of family, friends, seasoned parents, and professionals, we soon realized that it was essential to hold high expectations for Micah and to continue honoring our dreams—and most importantly his dreams.

> It is our dreams that fuel us, drive us forward, and pull us toward what has purpose and passion.

Early in Micah's life, we were fortunate to meet Marsha Forest, a brilliant educator and a bold leader in the inclusion movement (www.inclusion.com). One day, after listening to us describe our struggle to be the best possible parents to Micah, she sat us down for a pep talk. Her words were powerful and still guide us almost two decades later. She reminded us that the Rev. Martin Luther King Jr. shouted to the world, "I have a *dream!*" She paused, winked, and continued, "He did not say, 'I have goals and objectives.'"

Marsha reminded us to hold steadfast to our dreams, for it is our dreams that fuel us, drive us forward, and pull us toward what has purpose and passion. Of course, goals and objectives are useful in helping discover the next steps, but it is really the dreams, the visions of what can be, that compel us to take risks, to work harder, to reach out to others, and to hold on to even greater expectations for our child and our community.

Micah's journey into adulthood, with his intellectual disability, illustrates the importance of dreaming a life that is deliciously fulfilling. When he first started mentioning college at age 11, few would have believed that one day Micah would be part of the new wave of students with intellectual disabilities to be fully included on a college campus. His life is a constant reminder of what can be achieved when we "dream big," presume competence, and make the "least dangerous assumption" (Donnellan, 1984). (To read Micah's story, go to www.throughthesamedoor.com.)

Is It Denial, or Is It Hope?

Sometimes well-meaning professionals, while listening to parents talk about their dreams for their child, will refer to a parent as being "in denial" (Gallagher, Fialka, Rhodes, & Arceneaux, 2002). This certainly was the case when our son Micah talked about wanting to go to college. Students like Micah were typically enrolled in community-based vocational programs after high school, not in a university. After all, college was the place for students who read and write and are getting an advanced degree—not for someone with Micah's label.

During those high school days, when we were supporting Micah's dream to go to college, we were gently confronted by professionals who suggested that perhaps we were in denial, about Micah and his disability. My husband nodded as if he agreed, but surprised everyone with his tender and enlightening comment, "No, we are not in denial . . . not at all. We are definitely not in denial. We are . . . in hope. "

Indeed, being in the place of hope is essential to continuing the dance of partnership as well as the dance of parenthood.

So what is meant when the term "in denial" is used? Harry (1997), a parent and professor in special education, suggested that when professionals use the term "in denial" what they really mean is that the parents and professionals are "in disagreement" over the diagnosis, prognosis, or intervention plan. Disagreements are inevitable and require time, conversation, and deep listening. If we can reframe the phrase "being in denial" to "being in disagreement"; then perhaps the judge's wig will fall off and we can move into "being in discussion" with our partners, exploring a deeper understanding of all side of the issues.

In summary, there are numerous dance steps parents can practice, practice, practice. We've listed some of the most important. However, each family will discover which steps work best for them and for their child. What I [Janice] know as a parent of an adult with a disability, is that the steps of our dance repeat the following ideas

> Without these essential steps, the dance comes to a screeching halt. With them, the partnership succeeds and the child can dance the dream.

over and over: dream big, live in hope, believe in what you know about your child, build a circle of support, ask for help, learn more, and take breaks. Without these essential steps, the dance comes to a screeching halt. With them, the partnership succeeds and the child can dance the dream.

My Reflection: How does the reframing of "in denial" impact your thinking about what families might experience?

FOR PROFESSIONALS: ESSENTIAL STEPS

These essential dance steps for professionals will enhance their partnership with parents. The essential steps can be divided this way:

1. For all Partnerships: The Essential Steps
2. Preparing Parents: The Essential Steps
3. Beginning Meetings: The Essential Steps

4. During Meetings: The Essential Steps

5. Ending Meetings: The Essential Steps

We conclude with a poem written by Janice, who shares the importance of listening, the most basic and fundamental of all steps.

For All Partnerships at All Times: The Essential Steps

- Prepare yourself before talking or meeting with parents. You have a demanding schedule, and shifting from one activity to another requires concentration and intention. Do something simple before the interaction to remind yourself to *pause,* even if just for a moment. Take a deep breath, counting slowly back from 10 to zero, feel your feet on the ground . . . do whatever it takes to shift, to be present. Make this a simple ritual before every conversation or meeting.
- Remind yourself that it took you many years of study and practice to feel familiar with the laws, forms, procedures, policies, mandates, acronyms, services, and timelines. Reassure parents that it takes time to feel confident and comfortable with the information and process. Remind them that you are there to assist them.
- Be prepared for a range of feelings from parents, yourself, and others. Raising and teaching children is complicated and easily elicits a variety of emotions, often unexpected. The feelings can range from worry, fear of failure, uncertainty, joy, confusion, pride, and many more—sometimes all at the same time. Practice dealing with feelings and resist taking it personally when negative feelings emerge. Learning to handle strong emotions in yourself and others is as necessary a skill as knowing how to teach a child. Seek colleagues who listen to you with compassion, and who can provide support for handling strong emotions.
- Be aware of your body language and that of the parents. Ask yourself throughout the meeting, "Am I communicating openness in the way I am sitting, holding my hands, my shoulders, through my eye contact?" Remind yourself that 82% of communication is nonverbal (Stoddard & Valcante, 2000). Encourage parents to ask questions and to request

that answers be given clearly and with concrete examples. Assist parents in articulating their needs with such prompts as, "Sometimes parents want to know more about _____, while others want more information about _____. Do you have a preference?"

- Don't reassure parents too quickly. Well-intended statements such as "Everything's going to be fine" often feel dismissive and are experienced as a lack of understanding.
- Be mindful that when people appear agitated or "louder" that it is often a sign that they do not feel understood or heard. Step back. Speak less. Ask more open-ended questions. Write down the parents' issues, concerns and/or recommendations and ask if you have correctly captured their thoughts. Resist rushing to defend your position. Concentrate on obtaining more information from the parents.
- Ask parents what they have previously heard about the particular labels, diagnoses, services, plans, and experiences with early intervention or special education when there is tension or discomfort. Knowing the back story or the family's previous experiences or impressions might provide valuable insights and give you a new way to be helpful.
- Refrain from using jargon. If acronyms or technical terms are used, always provide an explanation and an example. Professionals new to the field might consider practicing the technique of sharing information with a friend or family member who does not work in the field of early intervention or education. He or she may then give you practical feedback about words to use or ways to explain. Provide a written list of commonly used words and their definitions. Parents and eventually children benefit when they are familiar with the terms frequently used, but they do not need to converse using the terms, especially during the initial phases and transitions.
- Strive to learn about the parent as a *person.* Inquire, with sincerity, about current happenings in the family such as an upcoming sports event, a family vacation or illness, or just about the daily routines. Ask parents how they are doing. Purposefully use "small talk" or simple chatting to ease into conversations and set a comfortable beginning.

> **My Reflection:** Name two other strategies you can use to promote partnerships.

Preparing Parents for Meetings: The Essential Steps

- Prepare parents about what to expect by contacting them at least a week or more prior to the meeting or conversation. Explain the purpose, length, and give an overview of the meeting; explain who will be there and what the parents should bring and what to be prepared to discuss. Encourage them to bring a list of their questions and priorities. Let families know they can bring someone to the meeting to take notes, be another listening ear, or to offer ideas and support.
- Offer parents options about ways to participate in the meeting if they can't be physically present, such as using telephones with speaker phones, video conferencing, Skype, written letters, and so on. (One father, stationed overseas, participated in his daughter's Individualized Family Services Plan meeting through Skype and web camera. It was a memorable experience for the family and providers as they gathered around the kitchen table.)
- Inform parents how to request a change in the date or time of the planned meeting and who to contact. Let parents

know what to do in case they are going to be unexpectedly late for the meeting or need to cancel at the last minute because of an emergency.

- Give parents the exact location of the meeting, where to park, which door to enter, who to see when they arrive in the building, and how they will get to the room where the meeting will take place. Let them know who will greet them. If you are doing a home visit, let families know how you typically meet in the homes and help them visualize the meeting. Help them feel comfortable about this arrangement and let them know it is an honor to visit them in their home.

- Create a sense of welcome before the meeting in your phone calls and letters. When mailing the formal or official letters to announce meetings, attach a sticky note to the letter with a short handwritten sentence or two, such as, "I'm looking forward to meeting with you, Mr. and Mrs. Schaeffer. I want to show you the great work Joshua did in math. Don't forget to call if you have any questions."

- Inquire about the need for an interpreter if the parents are deaf or hard of hearing or speak a language different from the providers. Some families prefer to have a family member or friend serve as the interpreter, but it is best not to use the student or a sibling. Make these arrangements before the meeting and include a discussion of the interpreter's role (Friend & Cook, 2010).

- Learn more about the diverse cultures of your community— and remember that every family has its own culture. Communicate an openness to learn from families about their values, influences, and traditions.

- Ask parents how they prefer to be addressed: Mr., Mrs., Ms., Miss, or by their first names. Do not refer to the parents by using "mom," "dad," and so on. Let parents know your preference in addressing you.

Beginning Meetings: The Essential Steps

- When parents arrive, let them know where the restrooms are located and offer them the opportunity to use the facilities before the meeting, especially if they have traveled some distance. Offer water or, when possible, tea or coffee. Before the meeting formally begins, set a comfortable tone by engaging in small talk, simple chatting, or inquiring about how they are doing. When you are visiting a family at their home, notice something inviting, positive, or unique about their home. Avoid having the professionals talking only to each other.

- Start with a warm welcome and introductions.
- Provide table tents or name tags with names and roles printed in *large* and *bold* lettering and provide the same for parents and visitors. This helps parents know every person's name and role. Some groups have laminated the table tents so that they can be reused.
- Share a few introductory comments, such as one of the following:
  - "Sometimes these meetings feel formal but we want to make them as comfortable as possible. We want this to be a time to share ideas, explore thoughts, ask questions, and get to know each other. We don't want forms to rule our conversations."
  - "There might be times during the meeting when we may not all agree immediately. Let's agree to slow down and explore the various ideas. It takes time and effort to create a shared understanding of the child."
  - "We encourage questions, lots of them. It's an important way to learn together."
  - "Remember, we can talk or meet again if more discussion is needed."
  - Ask that beepers and cell phones be silenced. If someone anticipates an urgent matter, provide the number of the secretary or other building personnel who can get the message to them. Place a "meeting in progress" sign outside the door to eliminate interruptions.
  - Set a positive tone. Do a quick round-robin asking each person to share a brief vignette about the child: "I noticed how Sam sucked out of his straw for the first time." "Rachel was so proud to show the photo of her new bike." "During recess, Michael asked Chandra to play four square."
- Invite parents to share what they know about their child, using their words. Encourage parents to share their own stories, give examples from their own home, and bring in photos.
- Help families explore their priorities, dreams, and expectations, and if needed, assist them in articulating them at the meetings.

My Reflection: What strikes you as important to remember when meetings are beginning?

Giving Information: The Essential Steps

- Begin with a few concrete examples of how the child demonstrated his or her abilities. Talk about what you enjoyed, noticed, or something unique about the child.
- Remind parents that together, you are discovering more about the child and that it takes time.
- If you are using standardized tests, have the materials ready for discussion. Provide a sample of the activities or questions asked and how the child responded or participated. Explain the meaning of a standard score as it is a common mistake to equate a standard score of 100 with 100%.
- Check for understanding frequently and clarify all areas of uncertainty. Vary how you inquire if parents have questions. Try asking: "What questions come to mind as we review this material?" "What feels confusing at this point?" Pause frequently, giving time for parents to formulate and ask questions, or to share concerns. Remember that silence is a necessary part of the conversation. Explain the meaning of the scores using concrete examples of how this data will inform the team about the best ways to support the child's growth and learning.
- Ask parents if the information sounds like their child. What doesn't make sense or doesn't fit?
- Remind parents that this type of assessment is only one way to understand the child. Provide information from other

assessment activities, including portfolios, anecdotal records, or observations (Friend & Cook, 2010).

- Ask parents, "What worries you the most? What doesn't make sense? What's the most important thing you've heard so far today? What do you want to make sure we know about your child?"
- When testing indicates that the child is eligible for special education services, carefully explain the rationale.
- Present and discuss the evaluation process, the assessments given, the professionals' reports, and the appropriate disability classification. Explain and discuss the definition of that classification and how the information gathered about the child fits the definition. If the information gathered fits more than one category, discuss both and determine as a team which classification is more appropriate.
- Listen carefully to the parents' questions and concerns. Give them time to reflect and opportunities to express their opinions.
- Ask if everyone at the table is in agreement. If not, stop and discuss.
- Present and discuss the special education services that will help the child. Discuss the various options and what each will mean in terms of the child's program. Encourage the parents to express their preferences.
- Clarify for parents that the label or classification in and of itself does not indicate what services and supports are needed. The services and supports are individualized and based on the child's strengths, needs, preferences, and interests.
- Work together and come to a decision. Again, ask if everyone at the table is in agreement.

Ending Meetings: The Essential Steps

- Summarize the major points discussed and decisions that were agreed upon. Identify any issues that need follow-up, who is responsible, and what are the timelines. Provide this in writing for the parents and the professionals involved in these tasks.
- Ask if there are any areas of disagreement and state the strategies or next steps that will be used to resolve the issue (Salend, 2011).
- Provide materials and resources for parents to take with them, such as *Parent's Guide to Special Education,* information on

procedural safeguards, and due process in their native language. Include a handout of resources on family-based groups from local, state, and national levels. Veteran parents or peer mentors can provide excellent support and information for families.

- Remind parents that they don't have to read all the materials immediately. In order to be sensitive to parents who might have reading challenges, offer, "Some parents prefer to read these materials on their own; others find it helpful when we go over it together. I can summarize some of it. Let me know what seems most helpful to you."
- Highlight a time during the meeting that exemplified effective problem-solving skills by the group.
- Encourage parents to follow up with any questions or concerns after the meeting.
- Encourage each person to share one final thought, question, or observation.

Begin and end meetings with intention and care. They are the bookends that hold together the stories, information, and plans discussed.

My Reflection: One thing I want to remember about beginning and ending meetings is

---

We conclude this chapter with a poem written by Janice when her son was first given a long list of labels (Fialka, 2011). She shares what it feels like to lose her child to labels and reminds professionals of the incredible gift of listening and supporting families.

Advice to Professionals Who Must "Conference Cases"

Before the case conference,
I looked at my almost five-year-old son
and saw a golden-haired boy
> who giggled at his baby sister's attempts to clap her
> hands,
> who charmed adults by his spontaneous hugs and
> hellos,
> who often became a legend in places visited
> because of his exquisite ability to befriend a few special
> souls
> who often wanted to play "peace marches"

And who, at the age of four,
went to the Detroit Public Library
requesting a book on Martin Luther King.

After the case conference,
I looked at my almost five-year-old son.
He seemed to have lost his golden hair.

I saw only words plastered on his face.
Words that drowned us in fear,

Words like:
> Primary Expressive Speech and Language Disorder,
> Severe Visual Motor Delay,
> Sensory Integration Dysfunction,
> Fine and Gross Motor Delay,
> Developmental Dyspraxia and RITALIN now.

I want my son back. That's all.
I want him back now. Then I'll get on with my life.

If you could see my worry
feel my sadness
Then you would be moved to return

our almost five-year-old son
who sparkles in sunlight despite his faulty neurons.

Please give us back our son
undamaged and untouched by your labels, test results,
descriptions and categories.

If you can't, if you truly cannot give us back our son
Then just be with us

quietly, gently, softly.

Sit with us and create a stillness

known only in small, empty chapels at sundown.

Be there with us
as our witness and as our friend.

Please do not give us advice, suggestions, comparisons or
another appointment. (That is for later.)

We want only a quiet shoulder upon which to rest our heads.

If you cannot give us back our sweet dream,
then comfort us through this evening.

Hold us. Rock us until morning light creeps in.

Then we will rise and begin the work of a new day.

MORE RESOURCES

To listen to Janice read *Advice to Professionals* and other poems and articles
http://danceofpartnership.com/

Special Education Resources on the Internet (SERI)
http://www.seriweb.com

Results Matter Video Library—Colorado Department of Education
http://www.cde.state.co.us/resultsmatter/RMVideoSeries.htm

US Dept. of Labor's website that the disability community to information and opportunities
https://www.disability.gov/

CHAPTER FOUR

When the Dance Is Complicated

A s evidenced throughout this book, partnerships are complicated and can be difficult at times. However, there are two particular situations—two types of dances—that are especially challenging and frustrating for professionals and make the partnership uncomfortable for parents, too. The first complicated "dance" we discuss is when parents appear angry. The second is when parents are absent or seem to be not involved—or not available. Our hope is that by studying the intricate steps in both situations the reader will enhance his or her understanding, compassion, and skills so that the partners remain in the dance, even when toes feel stepped on.

A COMPLICATED DANCE: WHEN PARENTS APPEAR ANGRY

Few of us know what to do when we come nose-to-nose with anger. Loud outbursts, shaking voices, and flushed faces disturb and frighten us and may trigger our most primitive impulses to freeze, fight, or take flight.

My Reflection: Think of a time in your own life when you experienced someone else's anger. Where were you? What did you instantly feel? What did you do or not do?

When faced with a parent who appears to be angry, professionals are likely to pull back, withdraw, or perhaps respond with harsh words of their own. They may wonder, "Do I really want to partner with this person?"

Consider the emotional scene in the 1983 film, *Terms of Endearment*, a story about the relationship between a mother, played by Shirley MacLaine, and her adult daughter, played by Debra Winger. In this scene, the daughter, who has three young children, is tragically dying of cancer. As she lies in the hospital bed in physical and emotional pain, she realizes she must make arrangements for her children's future. Her mother, MacLaine, sits helplessly at the bedside, and as agony contorts her daughter's face, she realizes that the nurses are late in administering the pain medication.

MacLaine hurriedly walks to the nurses' station and notifies the front desk nurse, "It's time for my daughter's pain medication. It's late. Please give it to her now." The nurse looks at her and says, "She's not my patient." Shirley storms from nurse to nurse, shouting, "My daughter is in pain. She needs her pain medication." Immobilized by the shouting, the nurses sit stunned. In sheer desperation, Shirley shrieks at the top of her lungs, *"Give my daughter her pain medication!"*

One nurse finally leaps from her chair and runs to the medicine cabinet.

> The key is to not be derailed by the anger, but rather to see it as an indicator that more patience and conversation are seriously needed.

Shirley notices the nurses staring at her in shock. In an attempt to gain back her dignity and reconnect with the nurses, she forces a stiff smile, takes a deep breath, slightly bows, and calmly says, "Thank you very much."

Most audiences feel tears flood their eyes.

When using this vignette in our training, we ask the following question to deepen the understanding of strong emotions such as anger: What is the mother (Shirley MacLaine) feeling at this moment?

My Reflection: List the feelings that the mother is experiencing at this moment.

Typical responses from the parents and professionals in the audiences include rage, powerlessness, desperation, anger, frustration, extreme anxiety, worry, helplessness, and panic.

We acknowledge these answers and then point out that one feeling is missing from the list. Take a guess.

The answer is *love.*

When audiences hear the word *love,* a collective sigh of insight quiets the room. With that awareness, it becomes obvious that Shirley's rage and desperate shouting come from her deep love for her adult child.

It is important for professionals to be mindful that the anger and other strong emotions expressed by parents are motivated by love for their child. Professionals don't have to feel comfortable with the anger, but they will be more effective partners when, instead of taking it personally, they understand that the anger is born of love complicated by many underlying factors. It might have to do with the current situation, but more likely, it is a result of unresolved issues or a feeling of not being heard. It might be related to the current school year, or perhaps it stems back to earlier years. It might even be connected to the parents' own personal experiences with school, social services, or how they perceive disability.

The key is to not be derailed by the anger, but rather to see it as an indicator that more patience and conversation are seriously needed.

Another Moment of Insight

After watching this scene from *Terms of Endearment* in a workshop composed of parents and professionals, a math teacher raised his hand and remarked, "I understand why the mother was raging in this situation—her daughter was dying. But the students in my classroom aren't dying; they do not have life-threatening disabilities. And yet so often I'm confronted by emotional, angry parents. I'm doing my best. Why are they so angry?"

At least 10 hands shot up in the air. The mother who was called on to speak composed herself and responded, "OK, you're right; my daughter isn't dying, but over and over again it feels that her dreams could die. As her mother, I feel I must stay alert and advocate for her constantly. It's up to me to keep her dreams and hope alive." With tears in her eyes, she turned to the math teacher. "I care so much, and it's just so hard. Can you understand?" He nodded and replied gently, "Thank you. I never thought of it in that way. I will listen differently."

It was a moment of truth and reconciliation, as both parents and professionals shared their deepest feelings.

Another Take on Anger

One of the authors (Janice) shares a personal story.

I once had a breakthrough during a school meeting when we were discussing my son's goals and objectives. As the teachers talked about his pre-reading skills, my unruly mind flung me into his distant future. At that moment, it was as if we were seeing two very different Micahs. While the teachers talked about Micah as a second grader, my thoughts fast-forwarded to Micah as a 30-year-old adult. Worries rained down on my heart. Would he have a home? A family? A fulfilling life? Would I have the energy to keep advocating for him for the rest of my life?

The teachers' concerns suddenly seemed trivial, and I blurted out something not very pleasant. To the team members at the table, my outburst must have appeared "out of nowhere." They were shocked and uncomfortable. Everyone looked away from me and a resounding silence filled the room. I was embarrassed. Why had I disrupted the meeting like that? The simple answer is, I couldn't help it. Emotion had welled up and out of me like a geyser. I needed to explain—and to understand it myself.

I cleared my throat. "You think that I'm angry . . . right? I must sound that way." I could tell I had their attention. "I don't think I'm angry . . . I think what I am feeling is . . ."

I frantically searched for the right word . . ."I am . . . terrified. That's it, terrified. About his future, about my inadequacies as a mother, the inadequacies of the school and of our community, and just overall terrified about the unknowns."

The silence continued, and I wondered if I had

> Anger can be scary and unnerving, but when it's honestly expressed and dealt with calmly, it can lead to deeper understanding and a stronger partnership.

totally blown it. Would they ever be able to relate to me? Would I ever be able to show my face at the school?

Then I noticed heads nodding and eyes meeting mine. Relief flooded through me. Not a lot was said at that moment, but there was a very different feel in the room—for all of us.

I shared what was on my mind and in my heart, perhaps not so eloquently as I would have liked, but with honesty. They listened and most seemed to understand. It was a powerful moment for me as a mother and as a person.

Another Take on Anger

One of the authors (Arlene) shares her personal story.

Looking back over my 20 years as Director of Special Education, I would have to say that most of my partnerships with parents were successful. This had a lot to do with communication. I tried to make sure that issues were discussed before they became problems, and that problems were resolved before they resulted in conflict. And while conflicts did emerge, they were ultimately settled and enabled us, as partners, to move forward.

I often noticed that parents *appeared* to be angry while experiencing other emotions, such as worry, fear, helplessness, frustration, or sadness. At other times, parents *were* truly angry, and this ranged from being upset or displeased to being irate, hostile, or even aggressive.

The reasons for their anger, all stemming from their love for their child, varied from parent to parent and situation to situation. Some parents were frustrated and felt that they were not being heard, especially in matters pertaining to their child's school, placement, or services. One father was furious that, even after hearing his preferences, the IEP team had recommended placing his 5-year-old daughter with Down syndrome in the neighborhood elementary school, rather than in a special school for students with disabilities.

Some parents felt that school policies were unfairly affecting their child and that the child's best interest was being ignored— like the mother, a single parent, who was irritated because the school district would not transport her son with a disability from school to her place of employment, which was located several miles away in a neighboring school district.

Some parents felt that they—and their parenting skills—were being blamed for their child's misbehavior. For example, one mother was incensed when family counseling was recommended after her first-grade son threw crayons and scissors at classmates, shouted profanities at the teacher, and knocked over a bookcase. In her eyes, the teacher was at fault for not controlling his behavior, and besides, he was "just being a boy."

Although it was often hard for me, I learned to stay calm and understand that the parent's outburst was not an attack on me personally. I focused on the issue at the source of the parent's anger, and really listened to what the parent was saying. I relied on the advice of other professionals, such as Jean Cheng Gorman (2004), a psychologist, teacher, and author of *Working With Challenging Parents of Students With Special Needs.* She suggests the following when faced with anger and strong emotions:

- Stay calm. Make sure your verbal and nonverbal communications manifest calmness. Your posture should be nonthreatening, your facial expression should be attentive and composed, and your voice should reflect your demeanor.
- Stay focused on the parent's primary concern and resist expanding the discussion to other issues.
- Find points of agreement—no matter how small—and use the words *I agree* . . . . "These two words are disarming and often end an angry tirade immediately because the parent no longer has to convince you of the injustice of the situation."
- Do not argue or try to prove that you are right.
- Do not get defensive and take things personally.
- Avoid making significant decisions and taking action when either partner is angry. "Decisions made in the heat of the moment are generally not the best course of action" (Kosmoski & Pollack, 2001).
- Remember that conflict is a normal occurrence in all relationships and should be used as an opportunity to gain a greater understanding of the issues.

My Recollection: If I remember only one thing from my reading about understanding anger, it is

I guess my behavior set the example for the other professionals with whom I worked—and the parents as well—because time after time, the heat of the moment subsided, and with understanding, patience, and effort, we were able to work out the problem together.

I'm not saying that anger is an easy thing to experience for any of the partners; it can be scary and unnerving, but I do believe that when it's honestly expressed and dealt with calmly, it can lead to deeper understanding and a stronger partnership.

Another Complicated Dance: When Parents Are Absent, Not Involved, or Appear to Be Uninterested

It's the evening of the "dance." One of the partners, the professional, is looking forward to gliding around the room with her partner, the parent. She has styled her hair, put on a new outfit, and slipped into her dancing shoes. She watches the clock, waiting in anticipation for her partner to appear at the door, and yet, as the minutes tick by, there's no sign and no call explaining the delay. She continues to wait . . . until she finally realizes that her partner is a no show. "Why?" she asks herself. "Why did my partner stand me up?"

Professionals sometimes experience similar situations with families. Standing ready and eager to help, they wonder why the family is not present at the meeting or why they didn't call with an explanation. In such situations, professionals feel baffled, frustrated, and in a quandary about what to do next. They struggle with understanding the "no show."

> Some parents might not realize that the professionals genuinely value their input, and want to work hand in hand with them.

In a recent education seminar, Arlene's graduate students brainstormed reasons why parents may not show at a meeting. Their list is worthy of consideration.

- They may not have transportation.
- They may not be able to get out of work.
- They may be ill.
- Their child may be sick, and they have no child care.
- They may feel that they don't have the "right" clothes to wear to a meeting.
- They may be stuck in traffic.
- They may have had a last-minute emergency at work or at home.
- They may have forgotten about the meeting.
- They may have been reluctant to drive in bad weather.
- They may have disturbing or troubling memories from their own time in grade school.
- They may have communication difficulties if English is not their first or dominant language and anticipate that being at the meeting would be frustrating or intimidating.
- They may have a conflict because of their other children's schedules.
- They may not have understood the importance of the meeting.
- They may not have a cell phone to call the school.
- They may be living in a homeless shelter and are embarrassed to discuss this with strangers.
- They may be living in a safe home and do not want to disclose their whereabouts.

Another important insight offered by Gorman (2004) is that some parents are not aware of the need for parent involvement and parent participation. Some parents might not realize that the professionals genuinely value their input, and want to work hand in hand with them to create a strong plan of action for their child.

Other parents might be intimidated by the process (*so many professionals, so many forms, so many unfamiliar terms being used*) or worried about the outcomes. (*What if they say my child has a disability? What if he needs special education? What if they think he needs a different school?*)

Another Story Comes to Mind

Diane, a graduate social work student, was placed in a middle school for her yearlong field experience. Her assignment was to work with 25 students with Individualized Education Plans. She carefully read each IEP, met with each student on a regular basis, had conversations with parents and staff, and diligently tracked each student's progress. Diane brought boundless energy, innovative ideas, a keen ability to build rapport with students and their families, and a passion to make big changes in the lives of her students. As she got to know the students, families, and community, she began to understand both their strengths and the challenges they faced.

Although parents weren't always able to attend meetings, she noticed that most responded to her upbeat phone calls and notes. Several even made plans to meet with her early in the morning.

However, there was one mother who, despite Diane's numerous attempts, did not respond to any of her messages. Early in the year, the principal and teacher consultant informed Diane that D.J.'s mother had never been involved in any IEP meetings or school events—ever. They cautioned her not to take it personally. "That's just the way it is. Focus on D.J. We've tried to connect with Mrs. Gibbs over the years, but nothing has worked."

Diane was not deterred. She was confident that her continued efforts would eventually get Mrs. Gibbs involved with the school. This year would be different for D.J. and his mother.

Diane felt a strong connection with D.J. because she, too, had been diagnosed with severe learning disabilities in middle school. She knew how frustrating it was to see letters on the page but have no idea how to *see* words and sentences. It was only with the support of a dedicated reading specialist and her own father's nightly homework help that she had learned to read. Over the years, she grew into a skilled advocate for herself and others, expertise she now hoped to share with D.J. and his mother.

After numerous phone calls and notes asking to meet with Mrs. Gibbs, Diane still had not received any response. The principal repeated his earlier advice: "Focus on D.J. His mother has never gotten involved." But Diane wasn't ready to give up.

After talking through her disappointment and concerns with her field supervisor, Diane decided that she would send home a brief handwritten note to D.J.'s mother every two weeks. Her notes did not pressure Mrs. Gibbs to respond or to meet with her. Rather, in each note, Diane shared a short anecdote about D.J. and an example of his work. She reviewed the notes with D.J. so that he understood their positive nature. Periodically, Diane included a photo of D.J. or a brief article about school events or parent information on learning disabilities and added, "I thought you might be interested in this."

Diane maintained her biweekly notes to Mrs. Gibbs, despite not hearing back from her for the entire year. When it came time for the end-of-the-year IEP meeting, Diane's note home listed a few suggestions for next year's goals and asked for Mrs. Gibbs's input. Diane hoped that Mrs. Gibbs would, at least, reply with some suggestions for next year or maybe—just maybe—Mrs. Gibbs would unexpectedly show up for the IEP meeting. To Diane's disappointment, this didn't happen. As usual, the meeting took place without family involvement.

As the year ended, Diane decided to send home a final note. In it, she included a photo of herself and D.J. holding the book he had written about his dog, Racey. Diane wrote, "I am glad I had the chance to meet your son. Thank you for sharing him. I also enjoyed writing to you. I will miss D.J."

On the final day of school, D.J. dropped off a crumpled note on Diane's desk. It read, "Thank you for sending me pictures of D.J. I liked the book about how parents can help their child read." The note was signed, "D.J.'s mom."

Diane stood quietly with the note in her hand. A connection had been made. Although she never got to meet D.J.'s mom, that little note was a big reminder to Diane to remain steadfast and respectful and to keep communication consistent and open—especially when it appears to be futile.

My Reflection: What are your thoughts about how Diane's communicated with D.J.'s mother?

A FEW OTHER POINTS TO CONSIDER WHEN PARENTS *SEEM* TO BE UNINVOLVED OR ARE ABSENT

Regrettably, not all families are comfortable having a connection with school. Although research and experience clearly tell us that home-school collaboration is ideal, it is important that professionals resist labeling parents as uninterested or "too busy to care." Parents are involved with their children in hundreds of ways that professionals may never see. If we were able to sneak a glimpse into the everyday moments, we would often see families being together, including those who never show at school events, meetings, or other activities. They might be cooking in the kitchen; sitting on the front porch; gardening; playing baseball at the corner field; participating at a church, temple, or mosque event; repairing a car in their driveway; watching movies; or visiting grandparents.

> Not all families are the same, not all families find school a safe place to be, not all families will be involved in similar ways.

The challenge for professionals, who understandably yearn for home-school relationships, is to remember that not all families are the same, not all families find school a safe place to be, not all families will be involved in similar ways. Of course, professionals strive to connect with families and to make schools inviting, safe places, but professionals need daily reminders that each family makes its own choices for its own reasons.

If we stay open to possibilities, we are less likely to make judgments about families—judgments that interfere with our ability to be as persistent as Diane was with D.J.'s mother. As Ann Hartman (1993), a wise social worker and professor, says, we must approach our work "with caution and humility."

Diane hoped that D.J.'s mom would surprise the team by coming to his IEP meeting. That didn't happen. Rather than giving up on Mrs. Gibbs, Diane remained steadfast, sending home one more positive note.

At the end of field placement, Diane's supervisor asked her, "What if D.J.'s mom hadn't sent you that note? How would you feel?" Diane sighed, glad that she didn't have to face that disappointment, and responded, "No doubt, I would have been disappointed and frustrated. But I would do it all over again. I thought it was important to stay in touch with D.J.'s mother, to keep letting her know that I care. It was the right thing to do, whether or not she ever replied."

Practical Suggestions to Encourage Parental Participation

- Remove the mystique of meetings (Gorman, 2004). Remind parents how important they are to the discussion. Once the meeting date is set, and parents have received their letter of invitation, send an informal reminder a day before the meeting by phone, e-mail, or note. Use encouraging words, "Dear Mr. and Mrs. Stein, We look forward to meeting with you tomorrow at 8:30 a.m. in Room 135. Don't hesitate to let me know if you have any questions or are having any

problems with getting to the meeting. My number is . . ."
Tell them that you are available to discuss any concerns,
worries, or questions *before* the meeting. Ask parents what
would help them feel comfortable at the meeting.

- Try to make contact with parents if they are later than 15–20 minutes. Use a tone of understanding: "I'm calling to see if you are able to attend today's meeting, or if you might be having any problems getting here. We just want to be sure that everything is OK" (Gorman, 2004).

> If parents regularly do not participate in meetings, keep the doors of communication open and your judge's wig off.

Keep the communication open. If parents regularly do not
participate in meetings, keep the doors of communication open
and your judge's wig off. We never know what might be
happening in the family. You can always offer, "I hope you can
make the next meeting" (Gorman, 2004), or in the case of Diane's
story, "Here's some good news about your child."

CONCLUDING THOUGHTS: WE ARE ALL PEOPLE FIRST

Gorman (2004) wisely reminds us that the "best way to ward off
nonparticipation" at meetings is to get to know someone on a
more informal or personal level. As shared earlier in this book,
focus on getting to know each other as people first. You don't have
to become best friends, but you can be friendly and show interest.
The following story illustrates this point. An early interventionist felt
she was not connecting well with a mother. The mother frequently
talked about how overwhelmed she was with four toddlers, two of
whom were receiving early intervention services. During one home
visit, the mother greeted the professional at her driveway. As the early
interventionist was getting out of her car, the mother happened to
look inside and noticed the backseat was piled high with children's
books, sports equipment, clothes, and bags of empty food packages
and water bottles. With a glint in her eye, she remarked, "Oh, you're a
normal mom too!" They shared a hearty laugh together. After that
unexpected encounter, the provider noticed a welcome shift in the

partnership—a connection was made, not between a parent and a professional but between two mothers.

 # MORE RESOURCES

Broadreach Training and Resources
http://www.normemma.com/

CONNECT: The Center to Mobilize Early Childhood Knowledge, FPG Child Development Institute, UNC
http://community.fpg.unc.edu/connect-modules

CHAPTER FIVE

Enhancing the Dance

Partnership Notes

Without music, there is no dance. Without communication, there is no partnership.

Communication between parents and professionals, between home and school, or between family and providers can take a number of forms. For example, parents and professionals, especially in early childhood and elementary school settings, often send notes back and forth in two-way notebooks as a way to update each other about a child's successes, struggles, and unexpected circumstances.

> *"Thank you for letting me know about the changes in Jose's medication. It helps to have a heads up. Jose had a great day in history class. He really seems to enjoy learning about the Civil War."*

"Mei-Ling might be a bit distracted at school today. Her sister was ill all last night, so she didn't get much sleep."

"Michael could use a bit more help on his math homework. He's struggling with the concept of subtraction. Thanks so much."

School professionals may also establish ongoing communication with parents of older students through the use of handbooks, orientation manuals, homework guidelines, and test preparation and study guides (Brandon & Brown 2009; Smith, Gartin, Murdick, & Hilton, 2006).

Spencer J. Salend (2011), noted educator and author of *Creating Inclusive Classrooms,* discusses other forms of useful ways to communicate:

- The informative notice, which alerts families about upcoming school and classroom activities, assembly programs, field trips, schedule changes, menus, and materials needed for upcoming projects.
- A class newsletter, frequently written by the students, which describes meaningful classroom activities and events that they've experienced.
- Daily or weekly progress reports, often mandated in Individualized Education Plans or Section 504 Accommodation Plans, which describe the student's academic performance, preparedness for class, effort, participation, classwork and homework completion, behavior, and peer relationships. As the student demonstrates success, the progress report can be shared with the parents weekly, biweekly, and then monthly.

Technological innovations have been changing the ways in which teachers, schools, students, and families interact and communicate (Ramirez & Soto-Hinman, 2009; Englund, 2009). Parents and professionals can use websites, e-mail, multilingual hotlines, Twitter, texting, interactive video conferencing, automated notification systems, and voice mail (Meadan & Monda-Amaya, 2008).

School professionals may communicate with families by maintaining a web log, which is a journal of the class' activities, and provide related web links found on the Internet. Online communication can be used by parents to support, communicate, and share information with school professionals and with each other (Margalit & Raskind, 2009; Meadan & Monda-Amaya, 2008).

If family members are unable to come to school for an important event, a video may be used to provide them with the opportunity of viewing the missed classroom activity, and to increase their awareness of their child's program (Salend, 2011).

PRACTICAL SUGGESTIONS FOR PROFESSIONALS

- Ask parents how they wish to communicate, and if necessary, find alternatives to written communication (Davern, 2004).
- Communication with families should be in a language in which they are fluent, preferably, in their primary language (Friend & Cook, 2010).
- When communicating with parents via technology, know that many parents might not feel comfortable interacting with you in that manner, or may not have access to various modes of technology. Therefore, rather than assuming a method of access, ask parents to identify the best ways for you to contact and communicate with them (Salend, 2011).
- Consider offering a workshop for families on the use of technology that can be used between home and school to enhance their comfort and skills.
- Increase the effectiveness of your written communication with parents by sharing factual information, avoiding the use of professional jargon and acronyms, providing examples, and emphasizing the positive (Fitzgerald & Watkins, 2006).
- Evaluate the written documents you send to families in terms of readability, legibility (if handwritten), tone, and use of clear, respectful, jargon-free language (Fitzgerald & Watkins, 2006). One way to check the tone of your note is to read it out loud and listen to how it might be heard by the receiver.
- Keep lengthy or sensitive communication about concerns and problematic issues to in-person or over-the-phone. E-mails and notes sent home that address more complicated matters can be challenging for families because there is no immediate opportunity for a back-and-forth discussion or clarification.

> Concrete feedback quiets the unresolved doubts ("Did I do this well?" "Was this OK to say?") and provides some reassurance and confidence that the dance is moving in the right direction for the child, the school, and the home.

PARTNERSHIP NOTES

There's another type of communication that we believe is equally important to enhance the working relationship. It's what we call "partnership notes"—feedback offered between parents and professionals about their work as team members. It is communication on a more personal level, offered by one partner to another about his or her involvement, contributions, or support.

Thanks for sending Jason the extra math homework. I appreciate your following through on our ideas.

Thank you for inviting our team into your home. I know that it was a very busy day for you, so we appreciate your willingness to spend time with us. We enjoyed getting to know your family. Delilah has such a happy giggle. We look forward to seeing you at the end of the month. Please don't hesitate to contact me if you have questions or other ideas.

It was thoughtful of you to find the software program on the solar system for our classroom. Ashley is having a great time with it and has enjoyed sharing it with her classmates.

I wanted to thank you for taking time yesterday to listen to my worries about Shaundra. I know I'll get through this difficult time. It helps to be able to talk about it with someone who knows the situation.

We are fortunate to have many avenues for communicating with partners even when we are not face-to-face. In addition to technology, children's backpacks can be handy communication conduits, and the post office still sells stamps for those old-fashioned handwritten notes. Everyone likes to find a cheerful card amid the bills in their mailbox or some words of appreciation in a string of e-mails. A warm and friendly telephone call can also work wonders!

Why Send Partnership Notes

Working and living with children who have disabilities has powerful rewards. It's also challenging work that demands the use of our hearts, minds, and souls on a daily basis. When parents and professionals receive honest and caring positive feedback from each other, it nourishes our commitment, informs us about what is helpful, and just plain feels good. Concrete feedback quiets the unresolved doubts ("Did I do this well?" "Was this OK to say?") and provides some reassurance and confidence that the dance is moving in the right direction for the child, the school, and the home.

One of the authors recalls sending a brief note to her son's kindergarten teacher telling her how much he was enjoying music class. The note read, "Micah's constantly singing, 'John Jacob Jingle Hammer Schmidt . . . That's my name too' as he dances through the house."

The teacher was delighted to receive this short but reassuring note. She had been troubled by Micah's quiet demeanor during class and wasn't confident that she was reaching him. This brief communication strengthened the teacher's understanding of the child and persuaded her to continue her efforts to engage him.

Partnership notes can reinforce working alliances by helping the partners learn more about each other's perspectives. Simple notes or e-mails can help parents and professionals know that they were heard. Additionally, by surfacing one's own hopes and concerns in caring messages, partners can make their visions for the child or the child's participation in the program more visible and more alive.

When to Send Partnership Notes

An excellent time to send a note of welcome is at the beginning of a relationship when parents and professionals initiate the dance of partnership. Recently, the mother and father of a young boy with autism approached their son's annual review meeting with apprehension. The past school year had been a difficult one, and the boy's parents were concerned about the upcoming year. They met their son's prospective teacher at this meeting and were delighted to receive the following note in the mail shortly afterward:

Dear Mr. and Mrs. Greenberg,

I enjoyed meeting with both of you yesterday at David's meeting. It's clear that he has two wonderful parents who are working hard to help him grow and develop! I look forward to our partnership next year, and I am excited about having David in my classroom! I know I'm going to learn even more about solar systems from him. Please call me with questions or concerns, etc.

Sincerely,
Linda Ojaye

David's parents are now approaching next fall with a renewed sense of hope.

Another mother gave her son's new fourth-grade teacher a poem she'd written about her son. The mother felt anxious and worried about the teacher's reactions to what she wrote. Her worry quickly vanished when she read the e-mail from the teacher, saying, "Thanks for sending me your poem. You helped me understand some of your experiences as a parent. I'm glad you shared it with me."

A letter, an e-mail, or a phone call can be made after a formal parent-professional meeting, such as an Individualized Family Services Plan meeting, an IEP meeting, a parent-teacher conference, or an informal exchange. Messages can also be meaningful when one member of the team is experiencing stress or a difficult time and the other partner recognizes this in a communication. When someone has made a positive contribution or a real effort to be helpful, a quick expression of appreciation helps the receiving partner feel valued. For example, this is the call that one father made to his daughter's teacher:

Hi Mrs. Jackson,

Thanks for taking Samantha and me on a tour of your classroom so she could get acquainted with her new room and new teacher. I know that the end of August, right before school, is a hectic time for teachers. We're looking forward to Samantha being in your class next school year. Please let us know if there is any way that Samantha's mom and I can be of help to you.

Feedback messages are also important in helping partners know what's working and what's not. For example, one mother left this message on her daughter's teacher's voice mail at school:

Hello, Mrs. Engle,

This is Mrs. Wilson, Maya's mom. I know that Maya has been having a hard time understanding the major ideas of the solar system. You've been patient and have really helped to break down the concepts for her. I have a good story to tell you. Last night, we stepped out on our back porch and Maya proudly pointed to the moon and said, "Really big craters!" She got all of us to look up and gaze at its wonder. Thanks!

When we encounter conflict or challenges in our communication, partnership notes can acknowledge the difficulties and address the desire to keep working together. A simple "I'm sorry" and other honest words offered to repair the relationship can help heal wounds. If left unspoken, feelings can fester and interfere with partnering.

One mother sent the following "repair note" via e-mail to her child's teacher after she had been particularly heated during a meeting.

> *Hello Mrs. O'Keefe,*
>
> *Thank you for listening so patiently to my frustrations about Courtney's difficulties in gym and at lunch. We want the school to help her learn to manage these times—and I guess some times we get overwhelmed. After our meeting with you, we thought of a few things we can do at home to support what you are doing in your class. Thanks for staying as calm as you did during the meeting. We'll keep working together.*
>
> *Thanks,*
> *Mrs. Mumen*

Partnership mail, as exemplified in the previous notes, calls, and e-mails, helps to make the unspoken thoughts between partners more visible. This type of communication has the potential to give depth to the working relationships that evolve between parents and professionals.

> The care and concern conveyed will be remembered for a very long time, and will motivate parents and professionals to persevere—to keep dancing.

Practical Suggestions for Sending Partnership Notes

The following are a few helpful hints for composing messages that will enhance the relationship between parents and professionals:

- Be brief, genuine, and authentic.
- Identify your partner's positive contributions. Be specific. Give examples.

- Convey your appreciation for the things your partner did *not* do or did *not* say for which you were grateful. Be clear about why the absence of these behaviors was helpful.
- Mention behaviors of which you would like to see more. Describe what your partner said or did and how you felt about it.
- Reframe the other person's difficult behaviors. For example, if the partner felt forceful in a meeting, acknowledge his or her positive intent: "I know you felt strongly about this idea. You are a strong advocate for your child. I admire that quality in you. Let's keep working on it."
- Take responsibility for your role in a difficult or tense interaction and apologize if that is appropriate.
- Include a statement or two about your expectations for the partnership in the future. Invite your partner to share his or her hopes and/or concerns.
- Remember to acknowledge feelings, stresses, and efforts.
- Although this kind of communication is important and meaningful, the recipients of partnership notes do not always respond to or acknowledge the messages they have received. This may leave the sender with a bit of uncertainty or disappointment. It might be helpful to remember that many people treasure, and even save the handwritten notes, e-mails, and phone messages they receive—even when they don't acknowledge their positive impact directly to the sender.
- Partnership notes need not be lengthy or time-consuming: a few words of care or gratitude, a lick of a stamp, a press of the "send" button on the computer, or a quick phone call are all it takes. The return on your investment through this kind of communication may be subtle and may take some time.
- Be assured that positive partnership notes build trust and goodwill. They can set the tone for an entire partnership, nurture every relationship, and help mend a challenging interaction. The care and concern conveyed will be remembered for a very long time and will motivate parents and professionals to persevere—to keep dancing.

My Reflection: Write a brief note to a parent or professional partner sharing something you valued or appreciate about him or her.

MORE RESOURCES

National Center on Parent, Family, and Community Engagement
http://eclkc.ohs.acf.hhs.gov/hslc/tta-system/family

Desired Results Access Project
http://www.draccess.org/videolibrary/

A Dance That Matters

The parent-professional partnership *is* a dance that matters because when the partnership is strong and the music is shared, our children do best and do *more*—more than we ever thought possible.

There's another, more personal reason to persist at building relationships with each other. Building partnerships has the potential to grow our humanity. Building partnerships requires us to listen; when it is hard to listen, to pause; when we want to leap in, to inquire; when we want to defend, to soften; when we want to attack, and to persist; when we want to turn away. This is no ordinary dance. This insight became more apparent to me during a conversation with my friend Kathy. I asked her, as an English teacher and eloquent writer, to read the first edition of the book and offer comments. After she read the book, we met for lunch. I sat with pen in hand, eager to record each of her suggestions. She took me completely by surprise when she simply remarked, "This is a book about kindness . . . kindness toward yourself and toward others."

This ingenious and insightful comment helped me to see the unintended soul of our book. Our motivation in writing this book was always about discovering ways to understand and promote partnerships. But as we listened to our stories and those of so many, we found other music—music that went deeper than the notes on the page, all the way down to the most fundamental requirements of human relationships: trust and time, and as Kathy put it, kindness.

This partnership building is not for the weary! It is demanding, serious, imaginative, ambiguous, unending, honorable, transforming work. What we have learned in writing this book, and will continue to relearn over and over, is that partnership building is also about growing ourselves, growing our own humanity, or as my wise 96-year-old mentor Grace Lee Boggs would say, "growing our souls and reimaging what it means to be human."

We conclude with the wisdom of Margaret Wheatley (2009), which condenses our book into just four sentences:

I believe we can change the world if we start listening to one another again. Simple, honest, human conversation. Not mediation, negotiation, problem solving, debate, or public meetings. Simple, truthful conversation where we each have a chance to speak, we each feel heard, and we listen well.

Resources for Families and Professionals

Throughout this book, we have encouraged families and professionals to seek resources to guide them in their decision-making process and to strengthen their knowledge. The task of sorting through the thousands and thousands of resources and materials available can be daunting. We offer the following short list. Though far from complete, each of the sites listed is highly recommended, reputable, user-friendly, and comprehensive and has a long history of serving families and professionals. In addition, several of the sites link to state-specific resources. We encourage professionals and parents to share this list with each other and the field at large.

The Beach Center on Disability
http://beachcenter.org

The Beach Center on Disability seeks to make a significant and sustainable difference in the lives of individuals and families affected by a disability by enhancing the partnerships with practitioners, policy leaders, families, and members of the communities. The Center bridges the gap between academic studies and the real-world 24/7 needs of families and individuals. The Center provides easy-to-use written materials, videos on important issues, communities of practice, training, and more. The Center is guided by its core values, which include supporting great expectations, making positive contributions, building on strengths, choice-based decision making, building relationships, and working toward equal citizenship for all.

The Council for Exceptional Children (CEC)
http://www.cec.sped.org

The Council for Exceptional Children (CEC) is considered to be the voice and vision of special education. It is a prominent association for professionals in the field of gifted and special education. CEC provides the latest information regarding research and practice as well as resources for teaching and learning. It seeks to improve the education and quality of life for children and youth with exceptionalities, and to enhance the engagement of their families to ensure that children and youth with exceptionalities are valued and full participating members of society.

Family Village Project
http://www.familyvillage.wisc.edu

The Family Village is a website for children and adults with disabilities, their families, and their friends and allies. Family Village brings together thousands of online resources in an organized, easy-to-use directory. The centerpiece of Family Village is the library, where visitors can find information on more than 300 diagnoses. Visitors can also learn about assistive technology, legal rights and legislation, special education, leisure activities, and much more.

National Dissemination Center for Children with Disabilities
http://nichcy.org/

National Dissemination Center for Children with Disabilities serves the nation as a central source of information on disabilities in infants, toddlers, children, and youth. Available at this site is easy-to-read information on the Individuals With Disabilities Education Act (IDEA), the law authorizing early intervention services and special education. State resource sheets connect to disability agencies and organizations in each state. Articles and publications, a newsletter, and more personalized assistance are available.

Parent Center Network
http://www.parentcenternetwork.org/parentcenterlisting.html

Parent Centers, comprised of Parent Training and Information Centers (PTIs) and Community Parent Resource Centers (CPRCs), provide training and assistance to the families of the nation's 7 million children with disabilities. These are funded through the U.S. Department of Education's Office of Special Education Programs (OSEP) under IDEA.

Every state has at least one PTI, and those with larger populations may have more. The CPRCs provide services to underserved families in smaller geographic areas. There are currently 106 Parent Centers in the United States.

Parent Centers serve families of children of all ages (birth to 26) and with all disabilities (physical, cognitive, behavioral, and emotional). Parent Centers provide a variety of services including one-to-one support and assistance, workshops, publications, and websites. The majority of Parent Center staff members and board members are parents of children with disabilities, so they are able to bring personal experience, expertise, and empathy when working with families.

Specifically, Parent Centers help families to

- Better understand their children's disabilities and educational, developmental, and transitional needs
- Communicate more effectively with special education, early intervention, and related professionals
- Understand their rights and responsibilities under IDEA
- Obtain appropriate services for their children through participation in the individualized education program (IEP) and individualized family service plan (IFSP) decision-making process
- Resolve disagreements and understand the benefits of alternative methods of dispute resolution
- Connect with other local, state, and national resources that assist children with disabilities

Parent Centers work collaboratively to improve outcomes for children with disabilities. They collect and share data from their work experience that lead to improved practices in serving children and youth with disabilities and their families.

Parent to Parent USA (P2PUSA)
http://www.p2pusa.org/

A national nonprofit organization committed to promoting access, quality, and leadership in parent-to-parent support across the country. This site highlights statewide organizations that have parent-to-parent support as a core program and demonstrate a commitment to implementing evidence-based P2PUSA-endorsed practices. The website includes a directory of state and regional Parent-to-Parent support organizations.

Institute for Patient- and Family-Centered Care
http://www.ipfcc.org/

The Institute for Patient- and Family-Centered Care, a nonprofit organization founded in 1992, takes pride in providing essential leadership to advance the understanding and practice of patient- and family-centered care. By promoting collaborative, empowering relationships among patients, families, and health care professionals, the Institute facilitates patient- and family-centered change in all settings where individuals and families receive care and support.

The Institute also serves as a central resource for policy makers, administrators, program planners, direct service providers, educators, design professionals, and patient and family leaders.

TASH
http://www.tash.org

TASH, an international leader in disability advocacy, works to advance inclusive communities and schools through advocacy, professional development, policy, information and resources for parents, families, self-advocates, and the professional community. Its publications, conferences, and webinars address a range of issues including best practices, family concerns, advocacy events, and policy change and include progressive research and breakthrough articles on inclusion, early childhood issues, positive behavioral supports, and disability issues of concern to families, students, self-advocates, and professionals.

The National Center for Family/ Professional Partnerships for CYSHCN
http://www.fv-ncfpp.org/

The National Center for Family/Professional Partnerships (NCFPP) promotes families as partners in the decision making of health care for children and youth with special health care needs (CYSHCN) at all levels of care. At this site, you can get more information on your local Family-to-Family Health Information Center (F2FHIC). The F2FHICs provide support, information, resources, and training around health issues for children and youth with special health care needs. Additional resources are provided at the end of each chapter.

References and Selected Readings

Alvarez McHatton, P. (2007). Listening and learning from Mexican and Puerto Rican single mothers of children with disabilities. *Teacher Education and Special Education, 30*(4), 237–248.

Angell, M. E., Stoner, J. B., & Shelden, D. L. (2009). Trust in education professionals: Perspectives of mothers of children with disabilities. *Remedial and Special Education, 30*(3), 160–176.

Araujo, B. E. (2009). Best practices in working with linguistically diverse families. *Intervention in School and Clinic. 45*(2), 116–123.

Bernheimer, L. P., & Weisner, T. S. (2007). Let me just tell you what I do all day. The family story at the center of intervention research and practice. *Infants and Young Children, 20*, 192–201.

Blue-Banning, M., Summers, J. A., Frankland, H. C., Lord-Nelson, L., & Beegle, G. (2004). Dimensions of family and professional partnerships: Constructive guidelines for collaboration. *Exceptional Children, 70*, 167–184.

Brandon, R., & Brown, M. R. (2009). African American families in the special education process: Increasing their level of involvement. *Intervention in School and Clinic, 45*(2), 85–90.

Checkley, K. (2008). Tapping parent and community support to improve student learning. *Education Update, 50*(4), 1–2, 4.

Davern, L. (2004). School-to-home notebooks. *Teaching Exceptional Children, 36*(5), 22–27.

Dettmer, P., Thurston, L. P., Knackendoffel, A., & Dyck, N. J. (2009). *Collaboration, consultation, and teamwork for students with special needs* (6th ed.). Upper Saddle River, NJ: Merrill/ Pearson Education.

Donnellan, A. M. (1984). The criterion of the least dangerous assumption. *Behavioral Disorders, 9*(2), 141–150.

Dunst, C. J., Herter, S., & Shields, H. (2000). Interest-based natural learning opportunities. In S. Sandall & M. Ostrosky (Eds.), Young Exceptional Children Monograph Series No.2: Natural Environments and Inclusion.

Englund, L.W. (2009). Designing a website to share information with parents. *Intervention in School and Clinic, 45*(1), 45–51.

Falvey, M. A., Forest, M, Pearpoint, J., & Rosenber, R. (1997). *All my life's a circle: Using the tools: Circles, MAPS & PATHS.* Toronto: Inclusion Press.

Fialka, J. (2001). The dance of partnership: Why do my feet hurt? *Young Exceptional Children, 4*(2), 21–27.

Fialka, J., Mock, M., & Neugart, J.W. (2005). *Whose life is it anyway? How one teenager, her parents and her teacher view the transition process for a young person with disabilities.* Waisman Center, University of Wisconsin-Madison. Available at http://www.waisman.wisc.edu/cedd/pdfs/products/family/WLIIAnyway.pdf.

Fialka, J. (2011). *It matters: Lessons from my son.* Huntington Woods, MI: Dance of Partnerships Publications (www.danceofpartnership).

Fitzgerald, J. L., & Watkins, H.W. (2006). Parents' rights in special education: The readability of procedural safeguards. *Exceptional Children, 72,* 497–510.

Floyd, L. O., & Vernon-Dotson, L. (2008). Using home learning tool kits to facilitate family involvement. *Intervention in School and Clinic, 44*(3), 160–166.

Fraenkel, P. (2006). Engaging families as experts: Collaborative family program development. *Family Process, 45,* 237–257.

Friend, M., & Bursuck,W.D. (2012). *Including students with special needs: A practical guide for classroom teachers.* Upper Saddle River, NJ: Pearson Education.

Friend, M., & Cook, L. (2010). *Interactions: Collaboration skills for school professionals.* Upper Saddle River, NJ: Merrill/Pearson Education.

Gallagher, P., Fialka, J., Rhodes, C., & Arceneaux, C. (2002). Working with families: Rethinking denial. *Young Exceptional Children, 5,* 11–17.

Gardner, H. (2006). *Multiple intelligences: New horizons in theory and practice.* New York: Basic Books.

Garcia, S. B., Mendez-Perez, A., & Ortiz, A.A. (2000). Mexican American mothers' beliefs about disabilities: Implications for early childhood intervention. *Remedial and Special Education, 21,* 90–102.

Ginsberg, M.B. (2007). Lessons at the kitchen table. *Exceptional Leadership, 64*(6), 56–61.

Gorman, J. C. (2004). *Working with challenging parents of students with special needs.* Thousand Oaks, CA: Corwin.

Harry, B. (1997). Leaning forward or bending over backwards: Cultural reciprocity in working with families. *Journal of Early Intervention, 21,* 62–67.

Harry, B. (2008). Collaboration with culturally and linguistically diverse families: Ideal versus reality. *Exceptional Children, 74,* 372–388.

Hartman, A. (1993). The professional is political. *Social Work, 38*(4), 365–366.

Hoff, D. L., & Mitchell, S.N. (2010). A peanutty dilemma. *Kappan, 91*(7), 59–63.

Ivey, A. E., & Ivey, M. B. (2007). *Intentional interviewing and counseling: Facilitating client development in a multicultural society.* Belmont, CA: Thomas Brooks/ Cole.

Janus, M., Kopechanski, L., Cameron, R., & Hughes, D. (2008). In transition: Experiences of parents of children with special needs at school entry. *Early Childhood Education Journal, 35,* 479–485.

Johnson, R. D. (2009). *Reaching out: Interpersonal effectiveness and self-actualization* (9th ed.). Boston: Pearson.

Knopf, H.T., & Swick, K. J. (2007). How parents feel about their child's teacher/school: Implications for early childhood professionals. *Early Childhood Education Journal, 34,* 291–296.

Koonce D. A., & Harper, W. (2005). Engaging African American parents in the schools: A community-based consultation model. *Journal of Education and Psychological Consultation, 16,* 55–74.

Kosmoski, G. J., & Pollack, D. R. (2001). *Managing conversations with hostile adults: strategies for teachers.* Thousand Oaks, CA: Corwin.

Kugler, E. G., & Price, O. A. (2009). Go beyond the classroom to help immigrant and refugee students succeed: School-based mental health services that partner with families to open doors to academic achievement. *Kappan, 91*(3), 48–52.

Lee, S., Turnbull, A.P., & Zan, F. (2009). Family perspectives: Using a cultural prism to understand families from Asian cultural backgrounds. *Intervention in School and Clinic, 45*(2), 99–108.

Lundquist, A. M., & Hill, J. D. (2009). English language learning and leadership: Putting it all together. *Kappan, 91,* 38–43.

Margalit, M., & Raskind, M.H. (2009). Mothers of children with LD and ADHD: Empowerment through online communication. *Journal of Special Education Technology, 24*(1), 39–49.

Matuszny, R. M., Banda, D. R., & Coleman, T. J. (2007). A progressive plan for building collaborative relationships with parents from diverse backgrounds. *Teaching Exceptional Children, 39*(4), 24–33.

Meadan, H., & Monda-Amaya, L. (2008). Collaboration to promote social competence for students with mild disabilities in the general classroom: A structure for providing social support. *Intervention in School and Clinic, 43,* 158–167.

Montgomery, D. (2005). Communicating without harm: Strategies to enhance parent-teacher communication. *Teaching Exceptional Children, 37*(5), 50–55.

Mueller, T. G. (2009). IEP facilitation. A promising approach to resolving conflicts between families and schools. *Teaching Exceptional Children, 41*(3), 60–67.

Naseef, R. A. (2001). *Special children, challenged parents: The struggles and rewards of raising a child with a disability.* Baltimore, MD: Paul H. Brookes.

National Youth Leadership Network. (2011). *Reap what you sow: Harvesting support systems.* Bethesda, MD: Author. [Materials available at www.nyln.org.]

Nelson, L. G. L., Summers, J. A., & Turnbull, A. P. (2004). Boundaries in family-professional relationships: Implications for special education. *Remedial and Special Education, 25,* 153–165.

Ohtake, Y., Fowler, S. A., & Santos, R. M. (2001). *Working with interpreters to plan early childhood services with limited English proficient families.* Technological Report No. 12 [electronic version]. Champaign-Urbana, IL: Culturally & Linguistically Appropriate Services (CLAS) Early Childhood Research Institute.

Olivos, E. M. (2009). Collaboration with Latino families: A critical perspective of home-school interactions. *Intervention in School and Clinic, 45*(2), 109–115.

Ramesh, S. (2008). Food allergy overview in children. *Reviews in Allergy and Immunology. 34*(2), 217–230.

Ramirez, A.Y., & Soto-Hinman, I. (2009). A place for all families. *Educational Leadership, 66*(7), 79–82.

Ray, J. A. (2005). Family-friendly teachers: Tips for working with diverse families. *Kappa Delta Pi Record, 41,* 72–76.

Rock, M. L. (2000). Parents as equal partners: Balancing the scales in IEP development. *Teaching Exceptional Children, 32*(6), 30–37.

Salend, S. J. (2011). *Creating inclusive classrooms: Effective and reflective practices* (7th ed.). Upper Saddle River, NJ: Pearson.

San Antonio, D. M. (2008). Understanding students and struggles. *Educational Leadership, 65*(7), 74–79.

Seely, K. (2005). The listening cure: Listening for culture in intercultural psychological treatments. *Psychoanalytic Review, 92*(3), 431–452.

Sheehey, P., Ornelles, C., & Noonan, M.J. (2009). Biculturalization: Developing culturally responsive approaches to family participation. *Intervention in School and Clinic, 45*(2), 132–139.

Sheehey, P. H., & Sheehey, P. E. (2007). Elements for successful parent-professional collaboration: The fundamental things apply as time goes by. *Teaching Exceptional Children Plus, 4*(2), Article 3.

Smith, T. E. C., Gartin, B. C., Murdick, N. L., & Hilton, A. (2006). *Families and children with special needs: Professional and family partnerships.* Upper Saddle River, NJ: Merrill/Pearson Education.

Sobel, A., & Kugler, E. G. (2007). Building partnerships with immigrant parents. *Educational Leadership, 64*(6), 62–66.

Stoddard, K., & Valcante, G. (2000). Families of children in elementary age services. In D. J. O'Shea, L. J. O'Shea, B. Algozzine, & D. Hammite. *Families and teachers of individuals with disabilities: Collaborative orientations responsive practices* (pp. 155–178). New York, NY: Allyn & Bacon.

Thomas, C. C., Correa, V. I., & Morsink, C.V. (2001). *Interactive teaming: Consultation and collaboration in special programs* (3rd ed.). Upper Saddle River, NJ: Prentice Hall.

Turnbull, A. P., Turnbull, H. R., Erwin, E. J., Soodak, L. C., & Shogren, K. A. (2010). *Families, professionals, and exceptionality: Positive outcomes through partnership and trust* (6th ed.). Upper Saddle River, NJ: Pearson. Coursesmart etextbook available at www.coursesmart.com.

Turnbull, H. R. (2011). *The exceptional life of Jay Turnbull: Disability and dignity in America 1967–2009.* Amherst, MA: White Poppy Press.

Ulrich, M. E., & Bauer, A. M. (2003). A closer look at communication between parents and professionals. *Teaching Exceptional Children, 35*(6), 20–23.

Van Haven, B., & Fiedler, C. R. (2008). Twenty ways to support and empower families of children with disabilities. *Intervention in School and clinic. 43*(6), 231–235.

Wadsworth, D., & Remaley, M. H. (2007). What families want. *Educational Leadership, 64*(6), 23–27.

Wheatley, M. J. (2009). *Turning to one another: Simple conversations to restore hope to the future.* San Francisco: CA: Berrett-Koehler.

Whitbread, K. M., Bruder, M. B., Flemming, G., & Park, H. J. (2007). Collaboration in special education: Parent-professional training. *Teaching Exceptional Children, 39*(4), 6–15.

Whiteman, N., & Roan-Yager, L. (2007). *Building a joyful life with your child who has special needs.* Philadelphia: PA: Jessica Kingsley.

Wood, R. A. (2009, January 15). Food allergies: Nothing to laugh about. *Los Angeles Times.* Retrieved from www.latimes.com.

CORWIN

A SAGE Company

The Corwin logo—a raven striding across an open book—represents the union of courage and learning. Corwin is committed to improving education for all learners by publishing books and other professional development resources for those serving the field of PreK–12 education. By providing practical, hands-on materials, Corwin continues to carry out the promise of its motto: **"Helping Educators Do Their Work Better."**